Here is Iran

Caricatures show the pure truth

Saman Taghizadeh

(Autor & caricaturist & painter)

I do not think so as the Iranian regime thinks. I consider this to be a difference. But the totalitarian regime does not tolerate any difference.

In my opinion

'Differences are beautiful.'

Copyright © 2017 Saman Taghizadeh

All rights reserved.

ISBN-10: **1977620728**
ISBN-13: 978-1977620729

CONTENTS

		page
1	Islamic university! what can I learn there?	1
2	Insurance & human	2
3	A wolf in our land	3
4	Oil-pool	4
5	They are allrounder; a representative of god	5
6	A killer called: Iran Khodro	6
7	**Inflation & Standstill**	7
8	Freedom of expression; You and your girlfriend	8
9	**Islam & Braindrain**	9
10	**Black execution**	10
11	**Human Rights & Islam**	11
12	**Demo**	12
13	**The devour our country**	13
14	**Nikah Mut'ah**	14
15	**A representative of god**	15
16	**...???**	16
17	**Dark and medieval of thinking**	17
18	**We are reach but poor**	18
19	**Dogs are impure**	19
20	**Dogs & Mullahs**	20
21	**God & oil**	21
22	**...??**	22
23	**Our fiend is...! Not west.**	23

24	Earthly paradise	24
25	…!!	25
26	What am I doing out of Iran?	26
27	God knows everything.	27
28	Heavenly justice	28
29	They never respect our people	29
30	Prohibited	30
31	Disunity	31
32	A Theater called: Voting	32
33	…!!	33
34	University in the West	34
35	Rockets	35
36	Demagoguery	36
37	…!!	37
38	Hanging	38
39	Rafsanjani	39
40	They feed themselves…	40
41	…!!	41
42	Iran has to be free	42
43	Holiday in Iran	43
44	God says…	44
45	Our Iran gets a grave	45
46	The Islam politics	46
47	Lebanon, Syria and …	47

1. ISLAMIC UNIVERSITY! WHAT CAN I LEARN THERE?

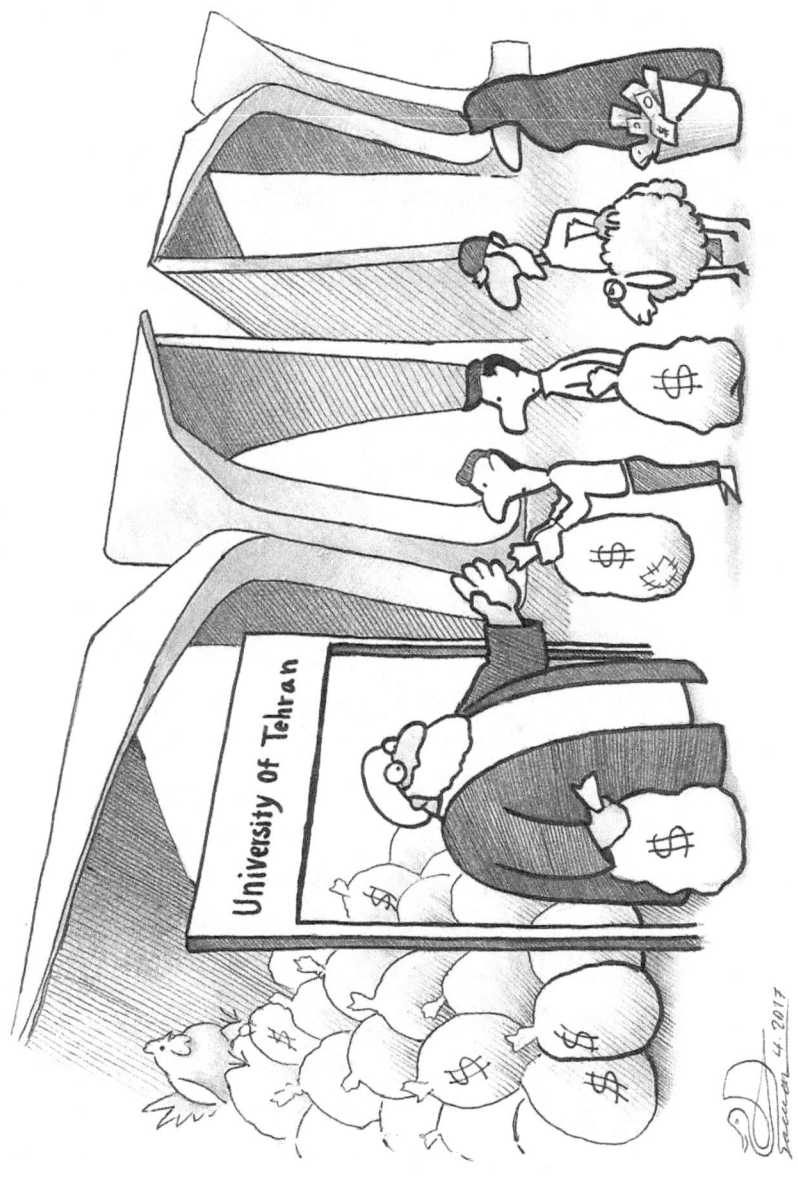

2. INSURANCE & HUMAN

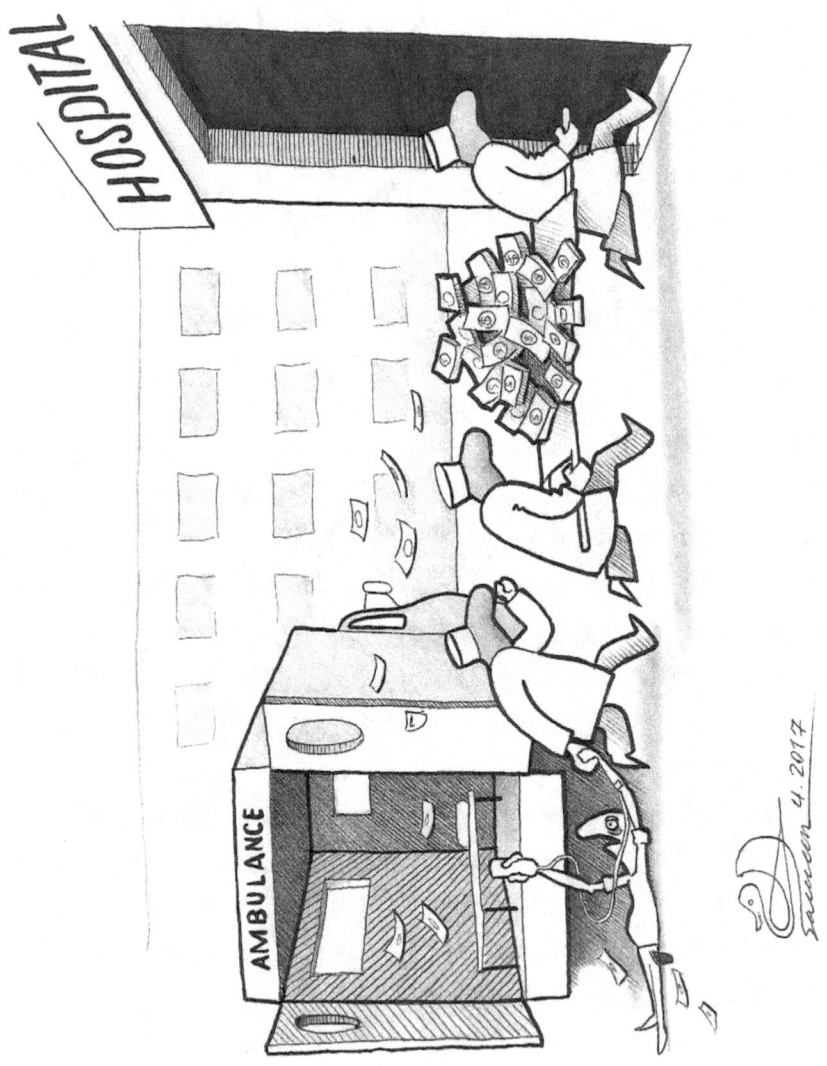

3. A WOLF IN OUR LAND

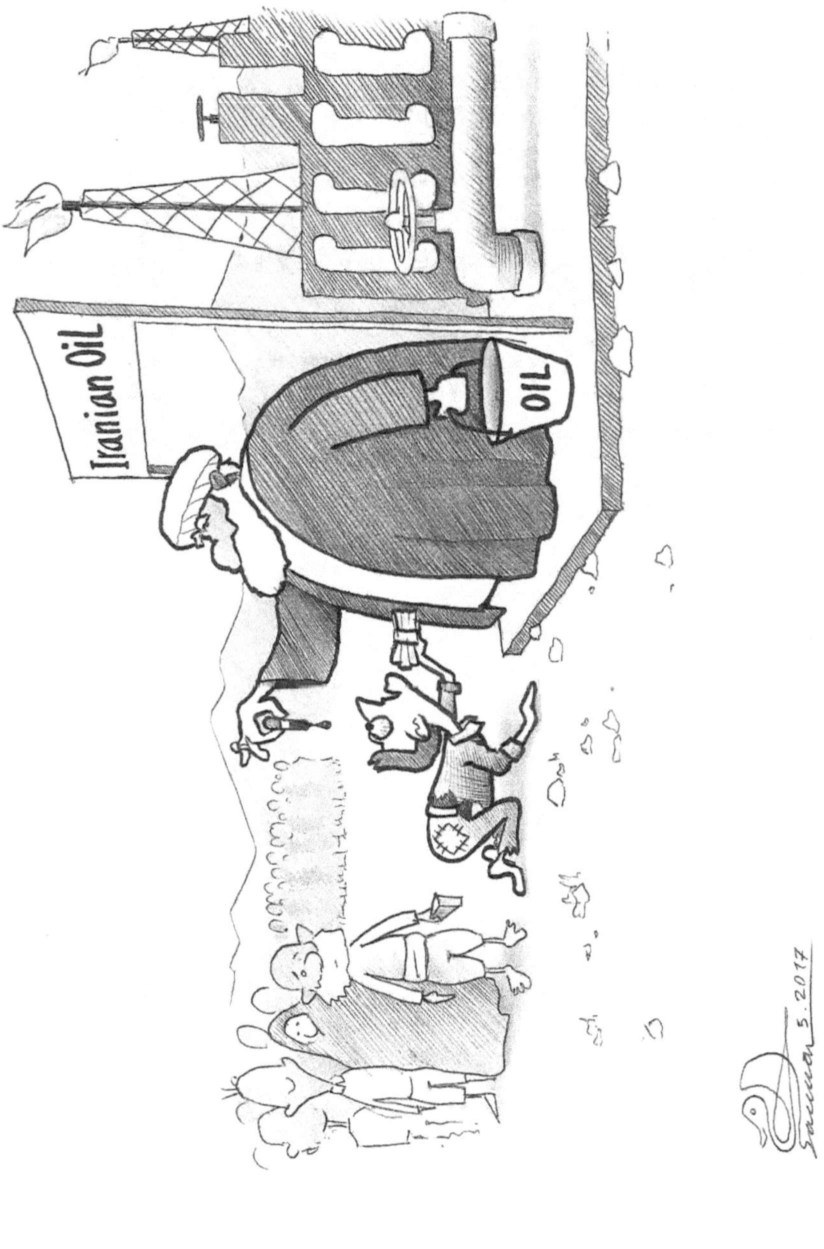

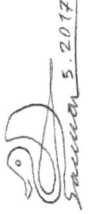

4. OIL-POOL

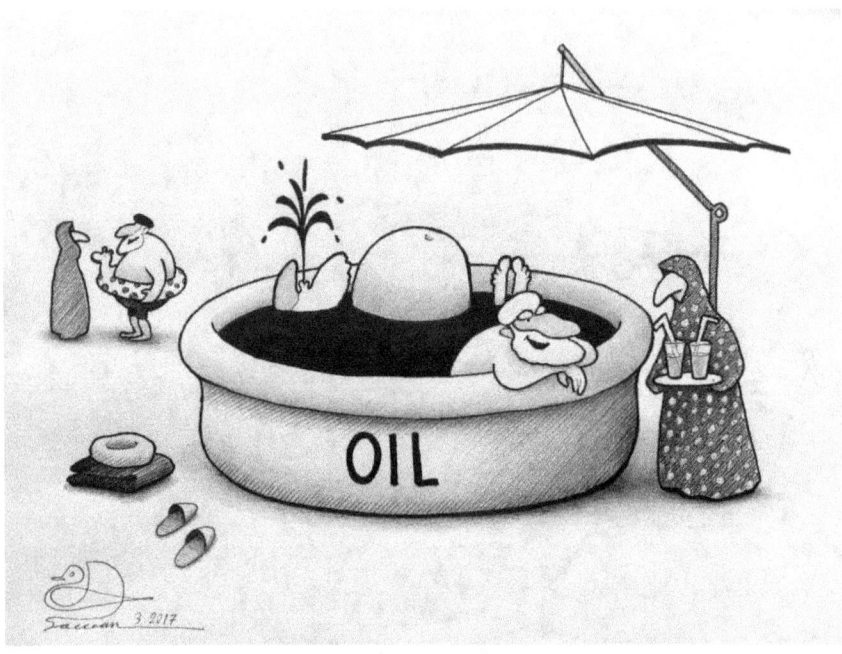

5. THEY ARE ALLROUNDER; A REPRESENTATIVE OF GOD

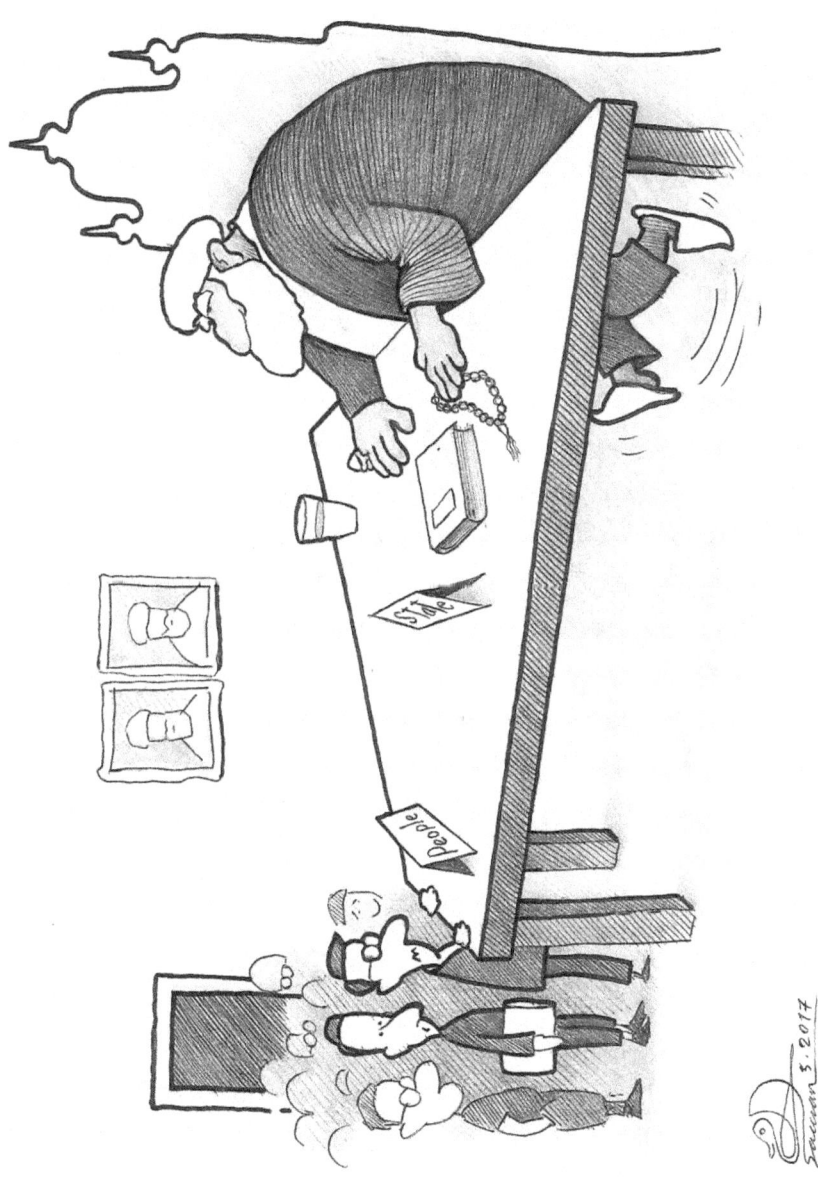

6. A KILLER CALLED; IRAN KHODRO
AN IRANIAN MULTINATIONAL AUTOMARKER

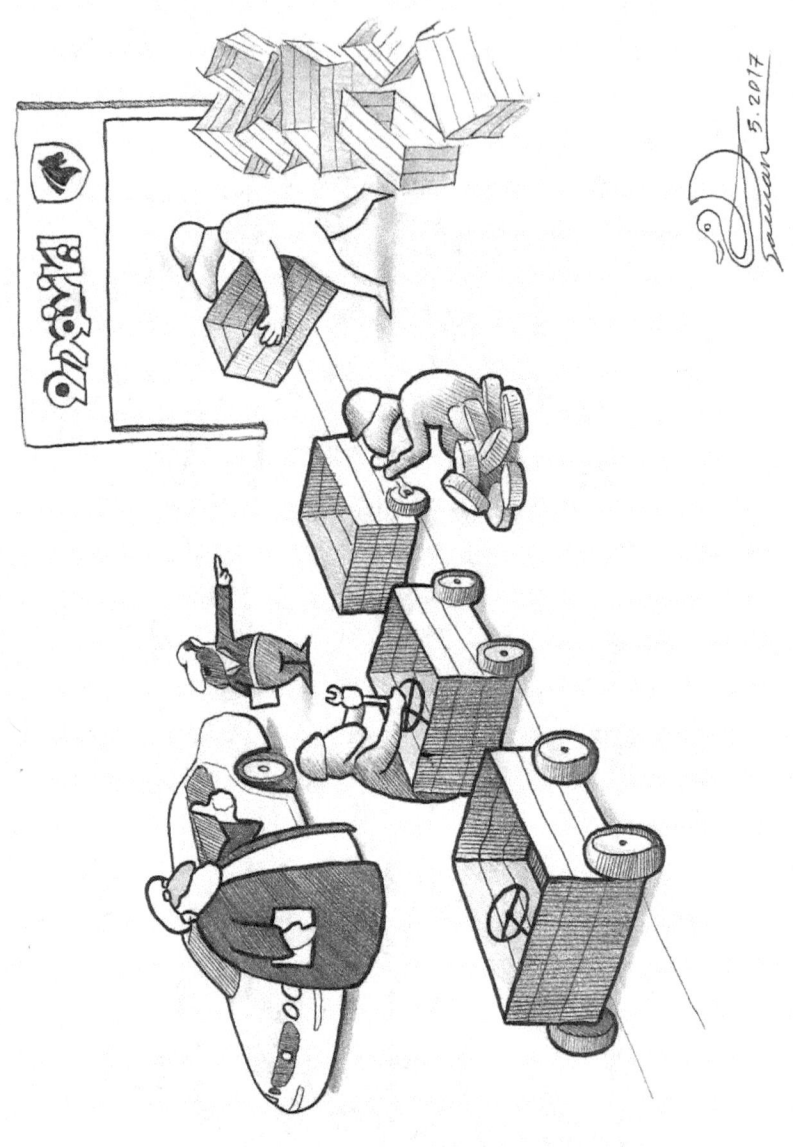

7. INFLATION & STANDSTILL

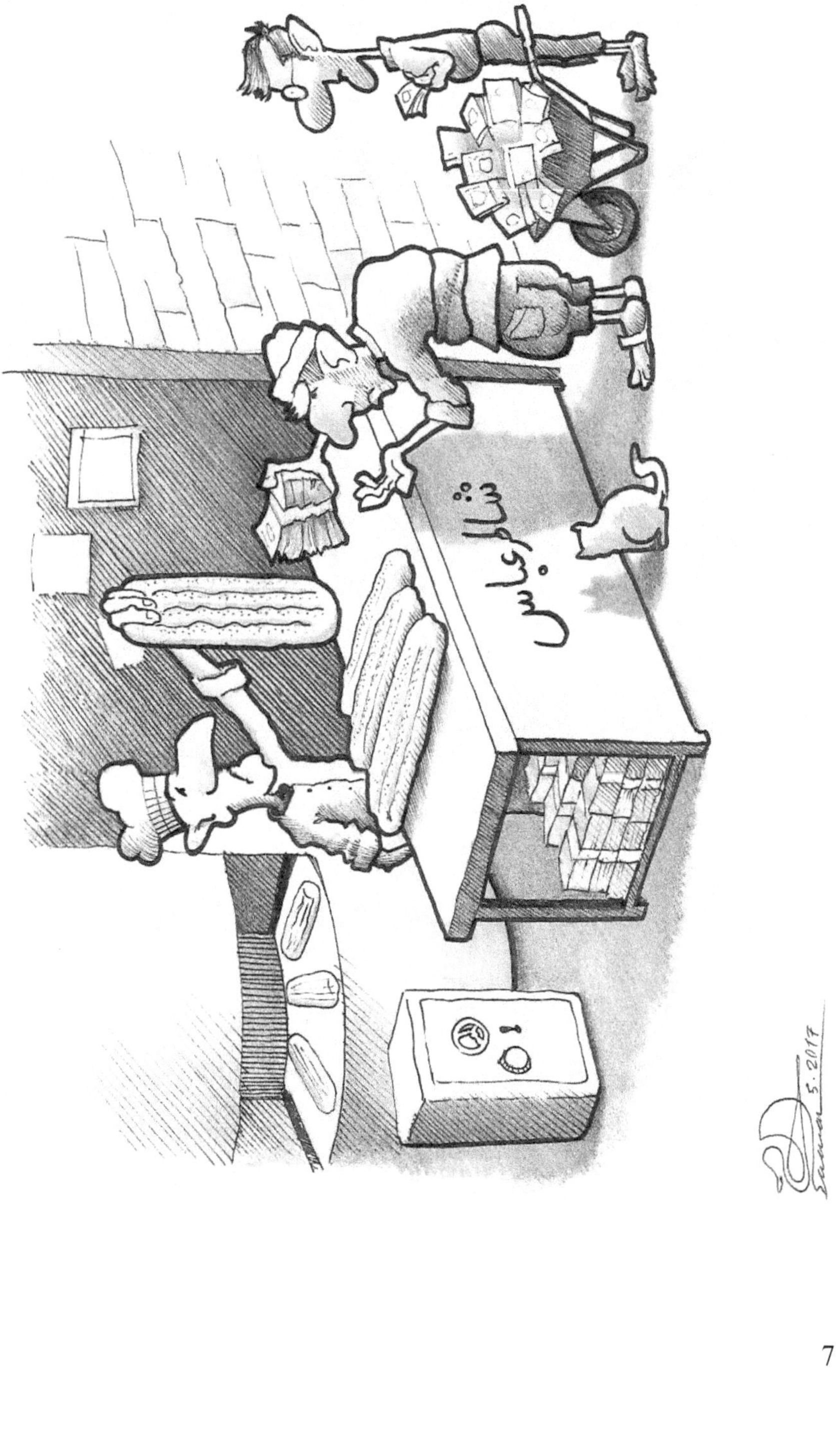

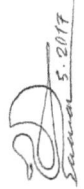

8. FREEDOM OF EXPRESSION; YOU AND YOUR GIRLFRIEND

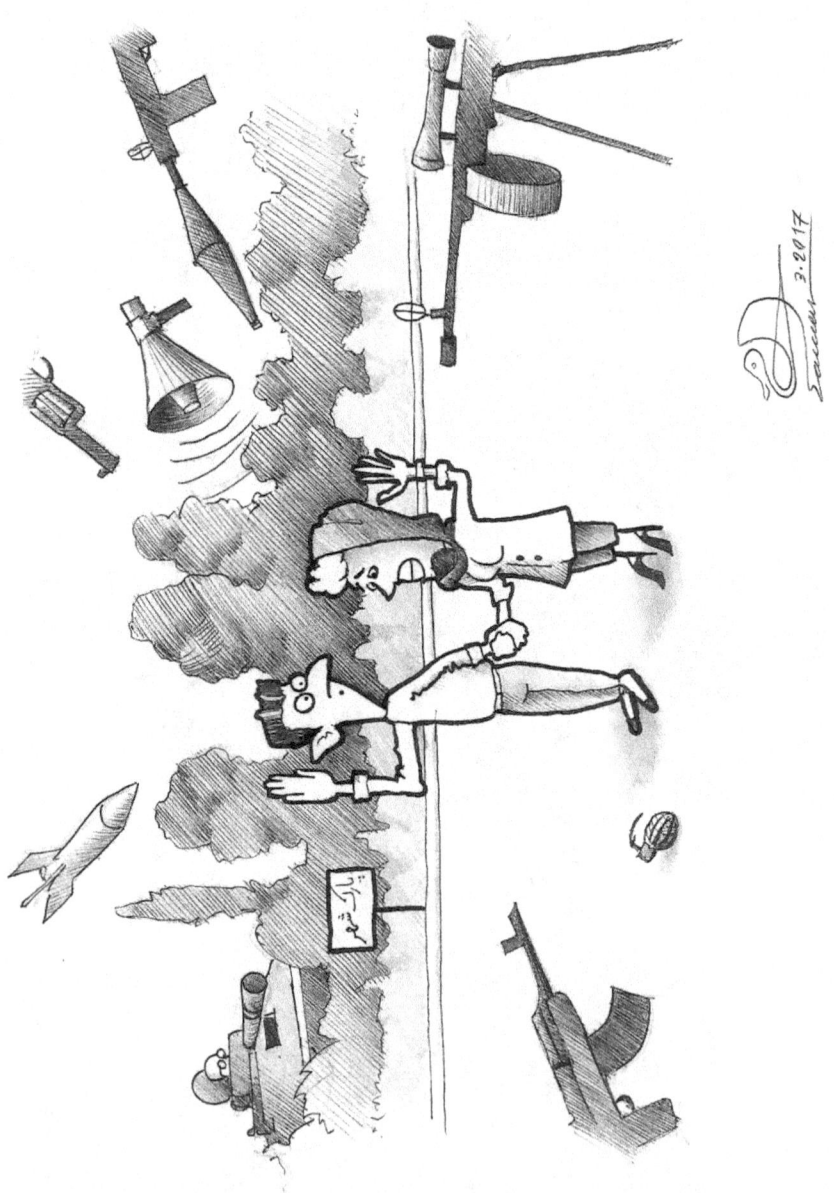

9. ISLAM & BRAINDRAIN
THAT DOES NOT BOTHER THEM

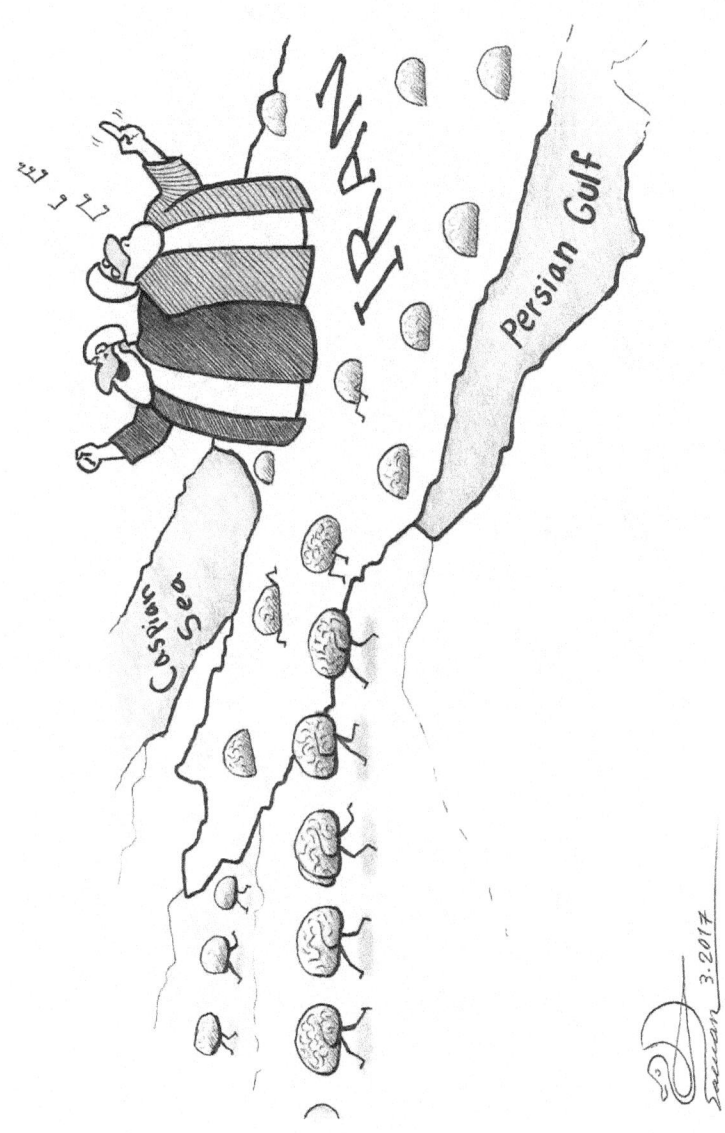

10. BLACK EXECUTION

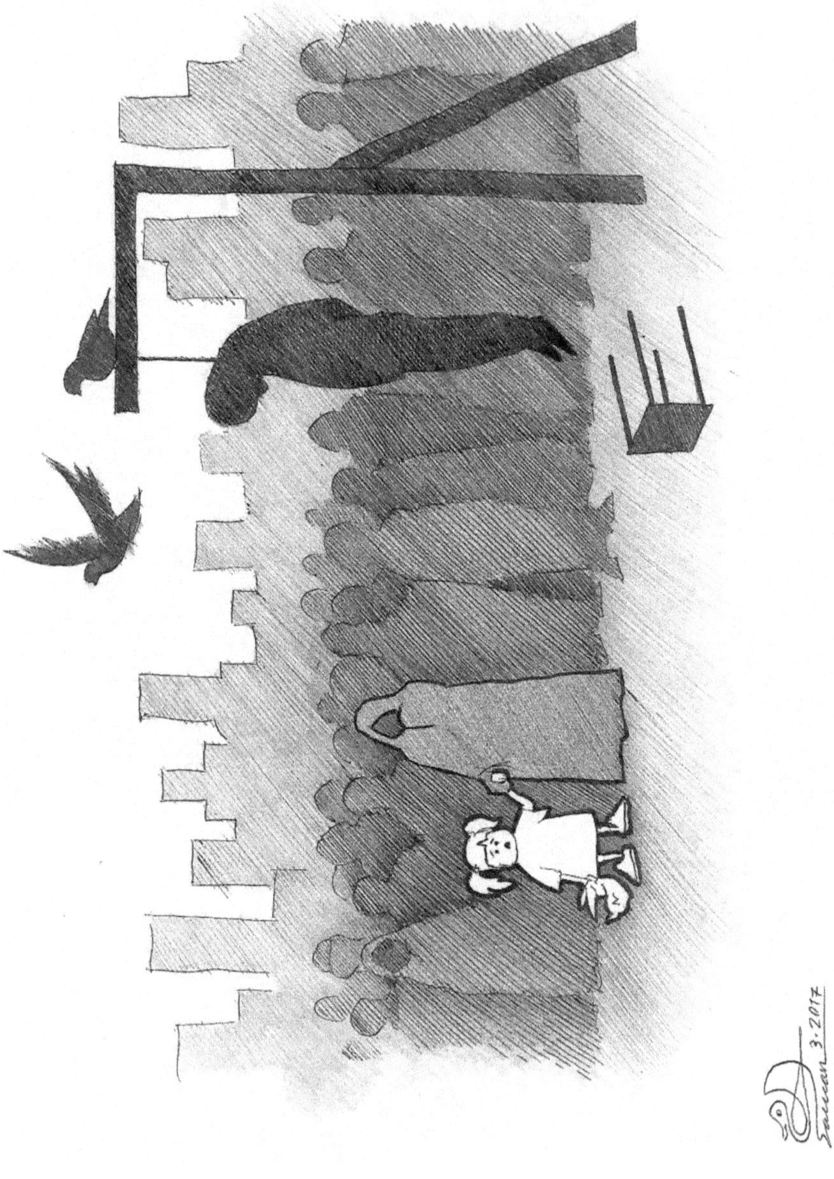

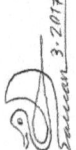

11. CHUMANRIGHTS & ISLAM

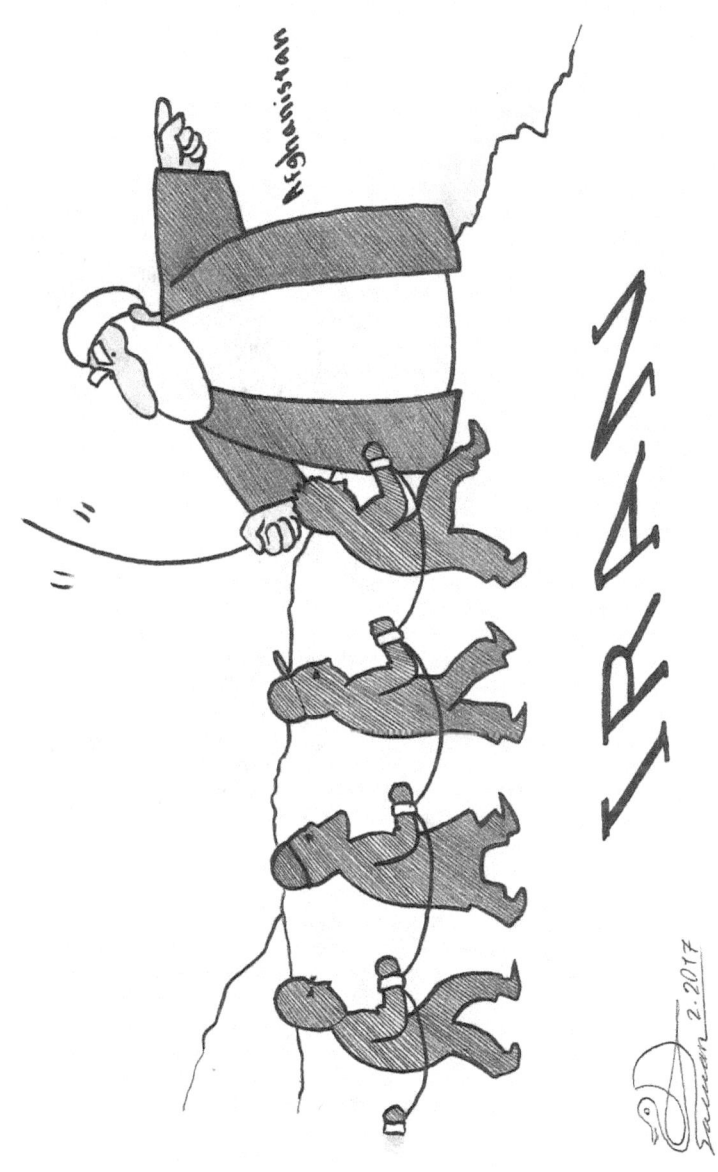

12. DEMO
A PACK OF PEOPLE AND NOTHING MORE

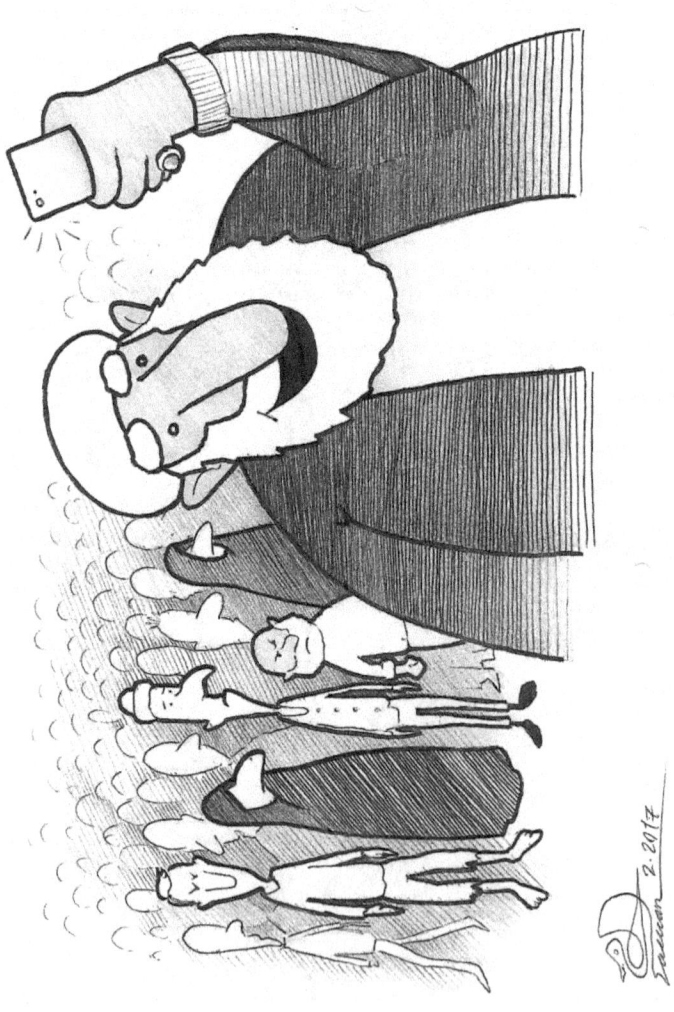

13. THEY DEVOUR OUR COUNTRY

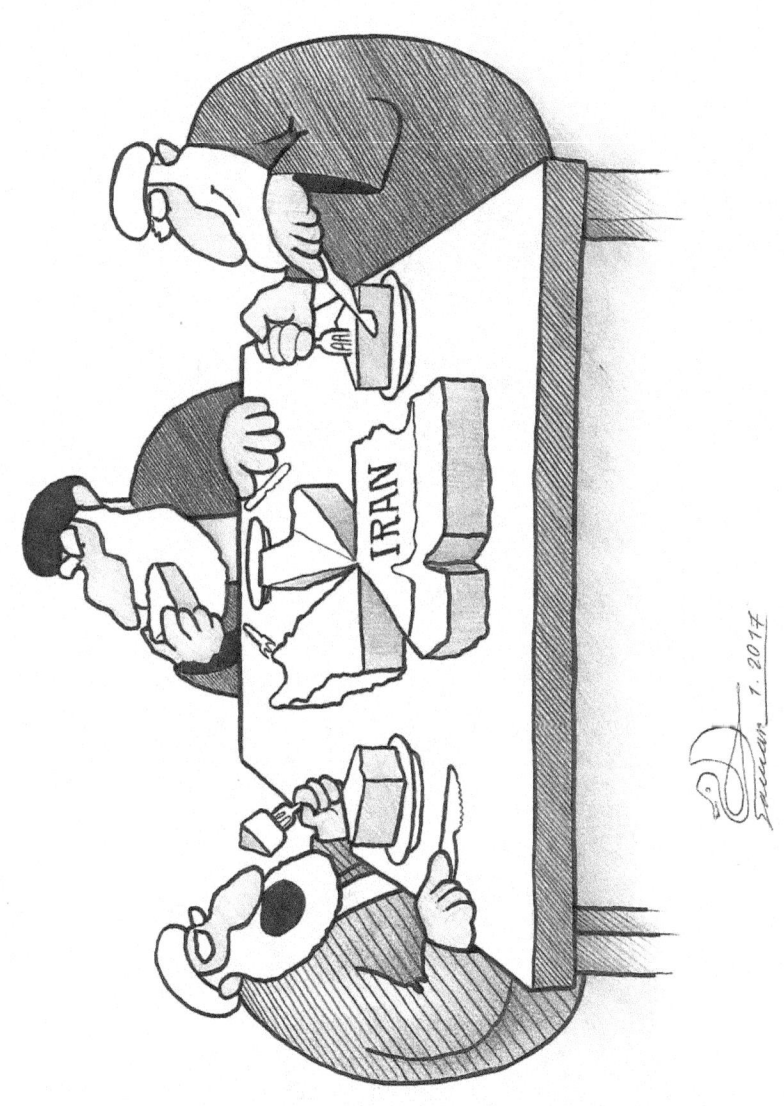

14. NIKAH MUT'AH
A VIOLATION OF WOME 'S RIGHT

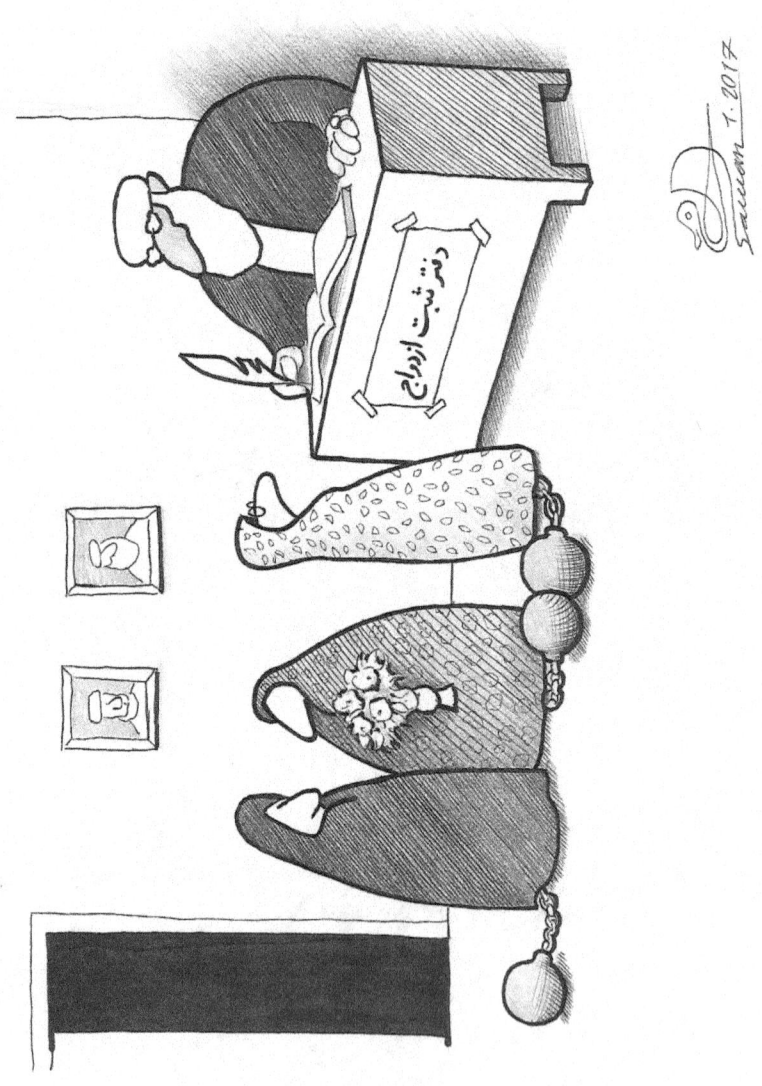

15. A REPRESENTATIVE OF GOD IS DOMINANT

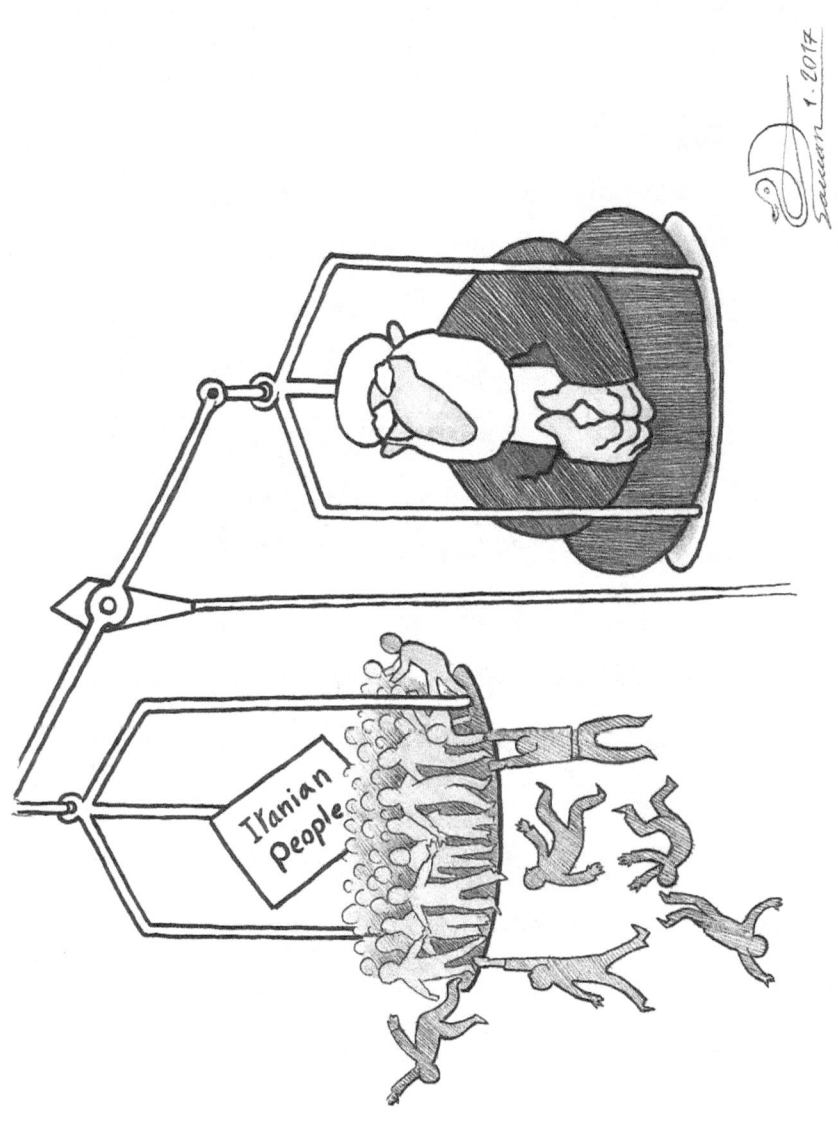

16. ???

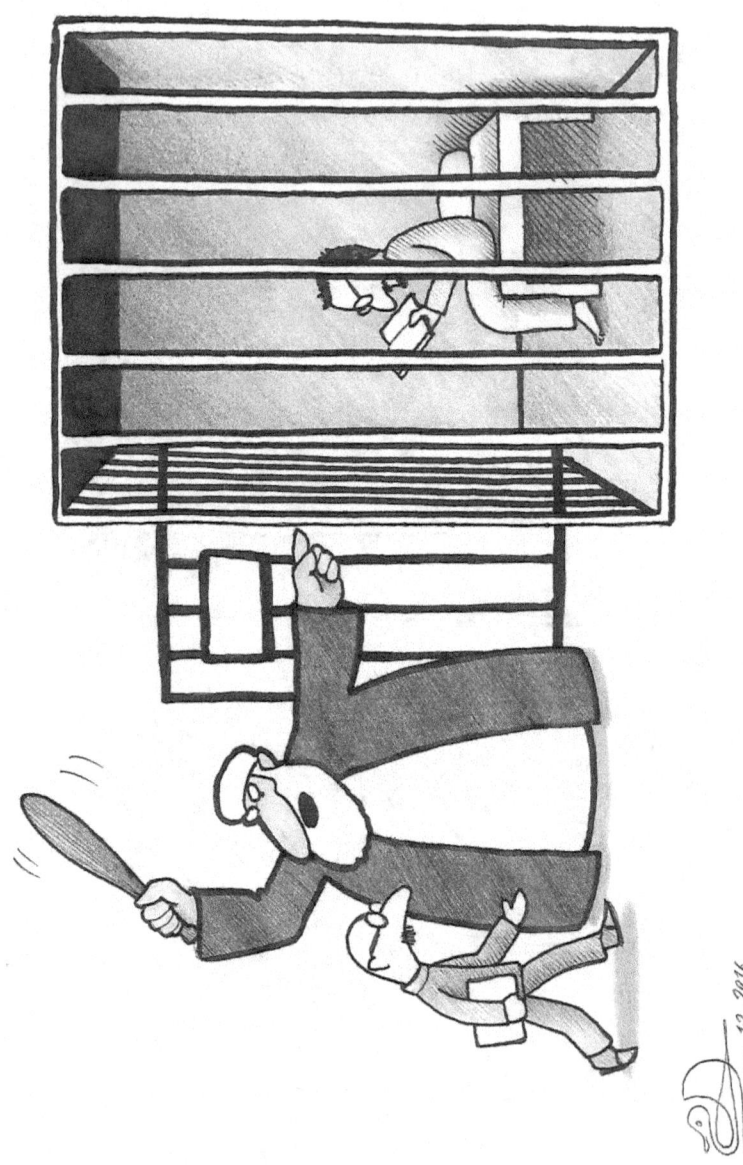

17. DARK AND MEDIEVAL OF THINKING

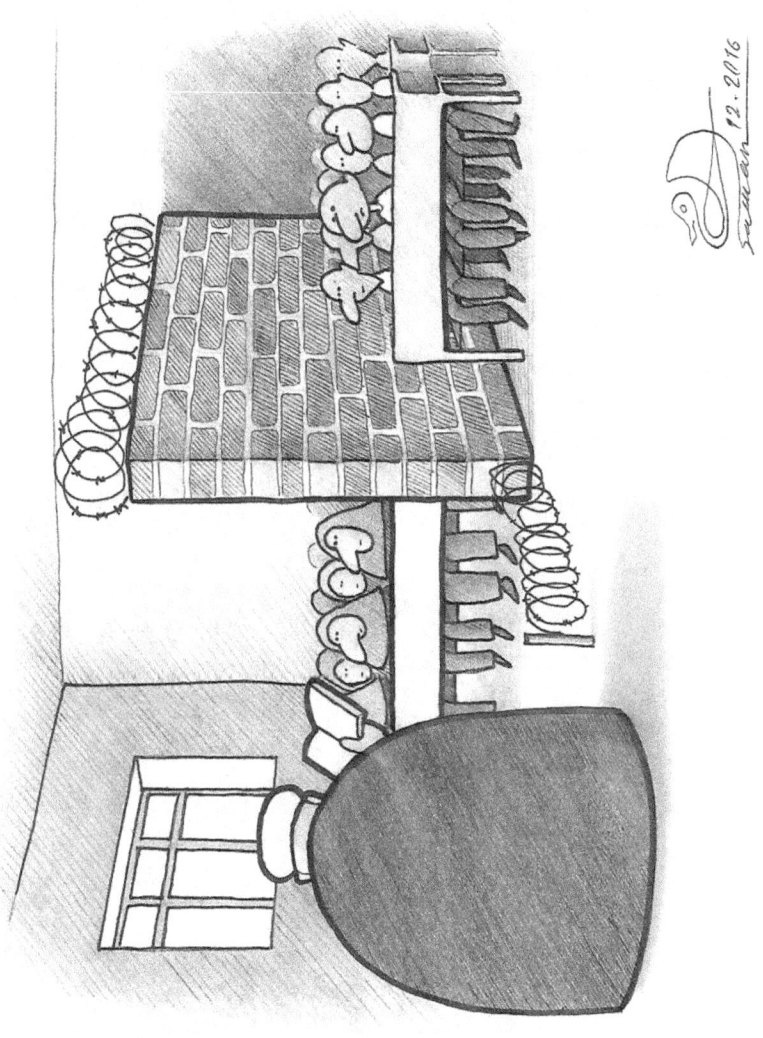

18. WE ARE REACH BUT POOR

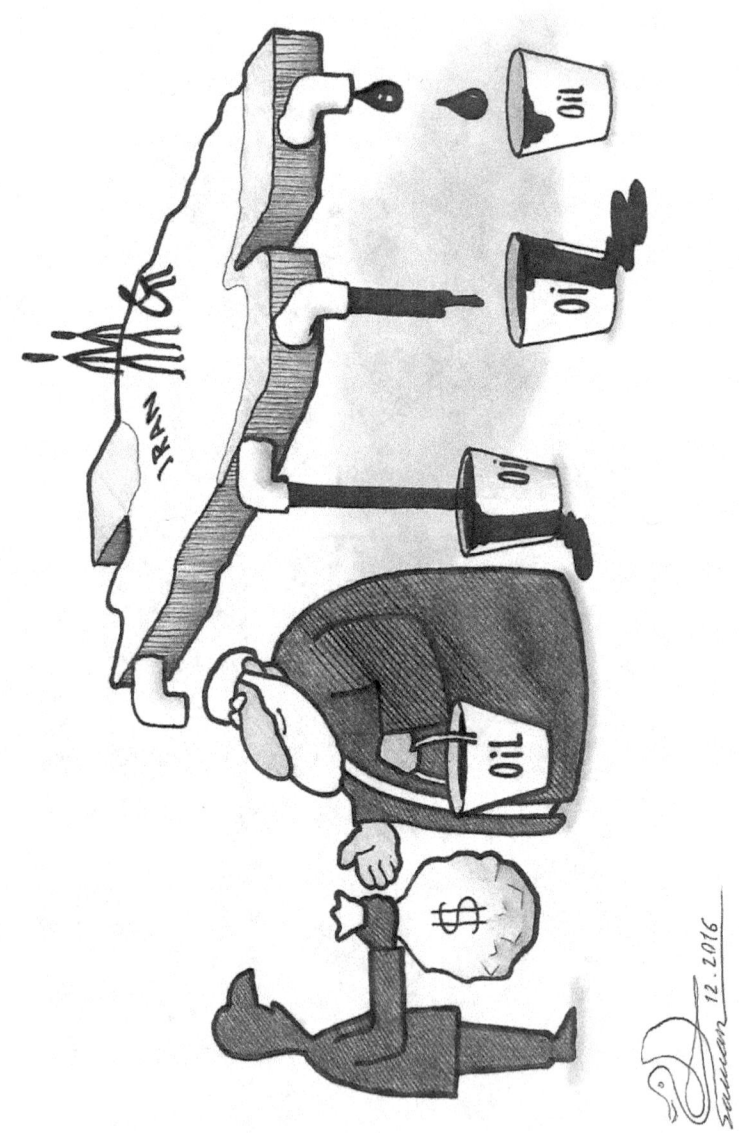

19. DOGS ARE IMPURE

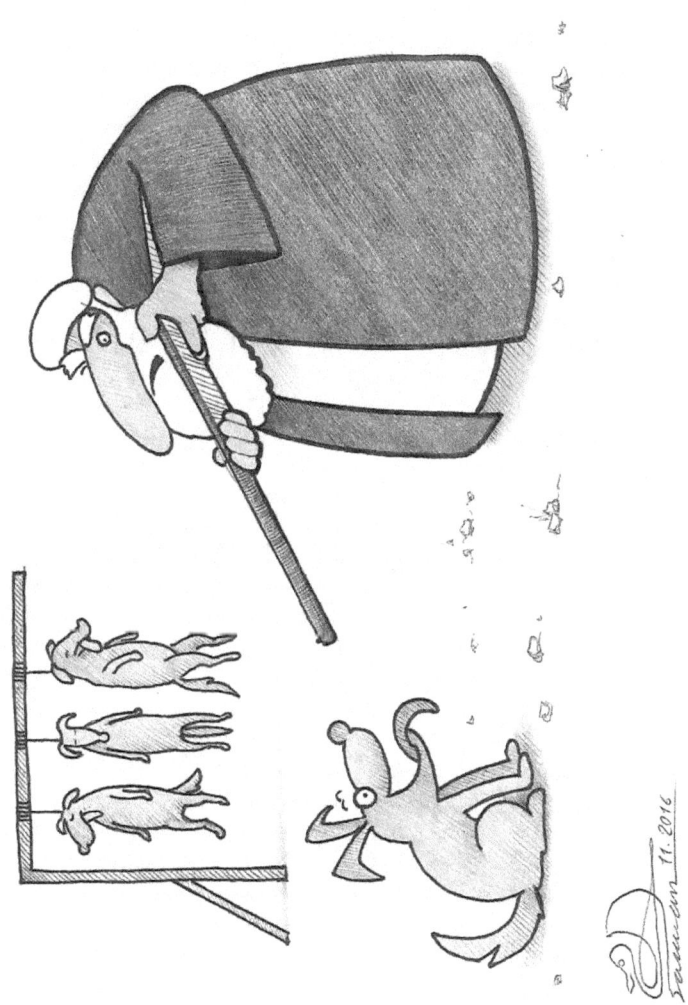

20. DOG & MULLAHS

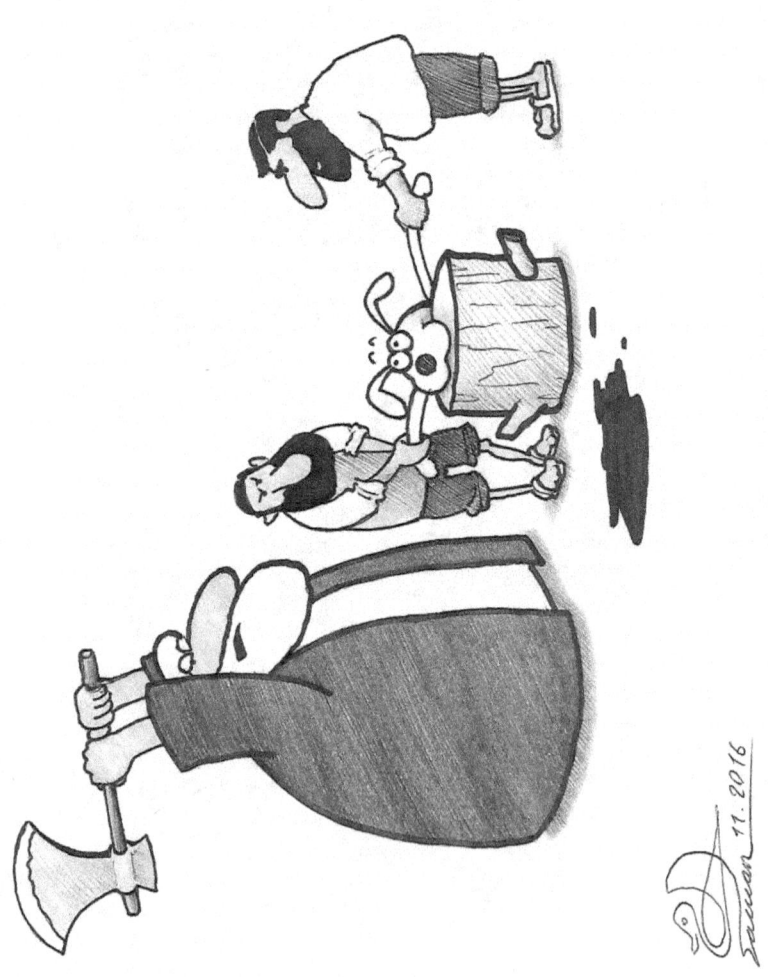

21. GOD & OIL!

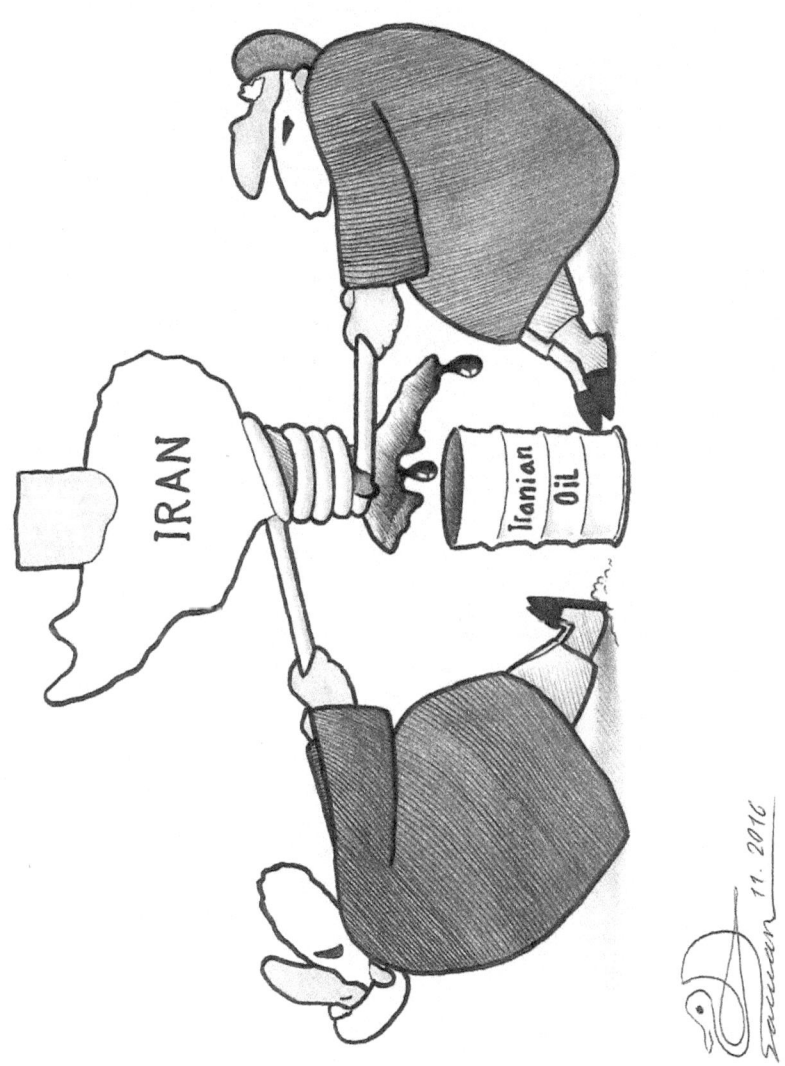

22. ???

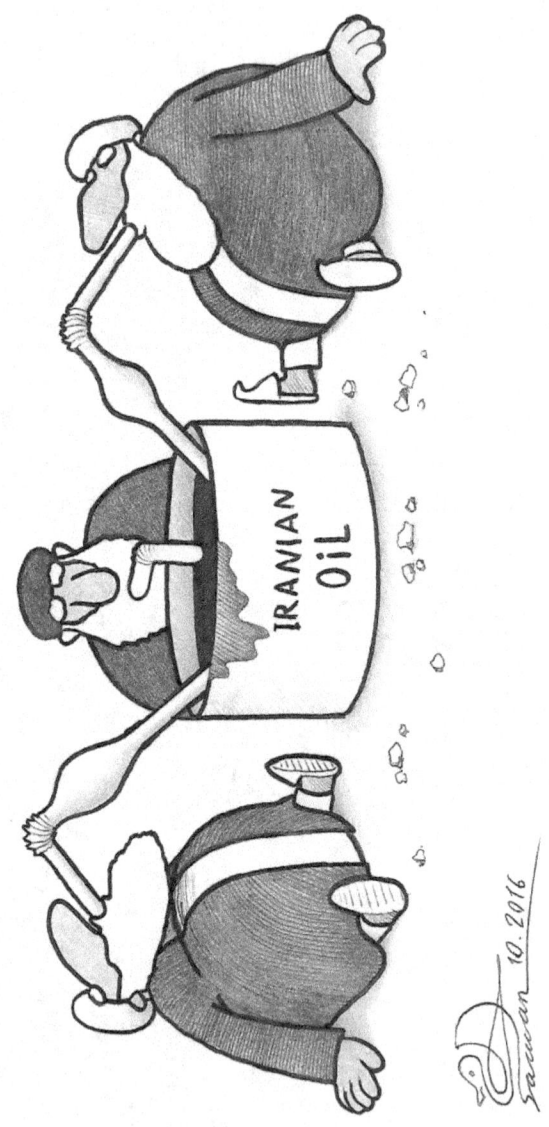

23. OUR FIEND IST … ! NOT WEST !

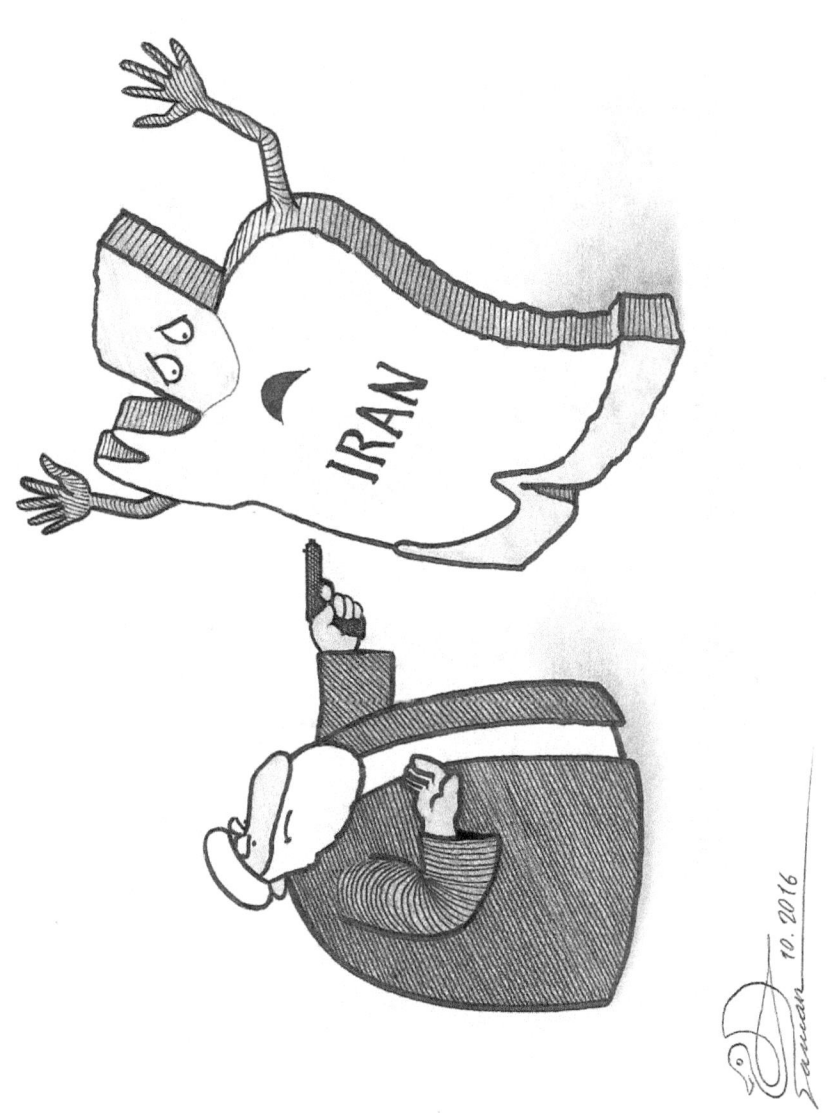

24. EARTHLY PARADISE

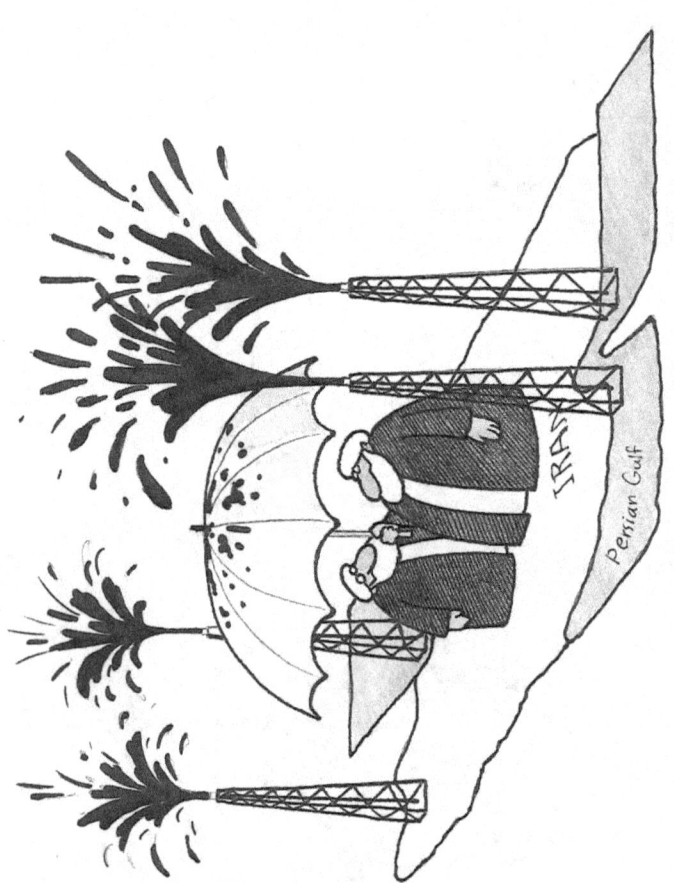

25. ….!!!

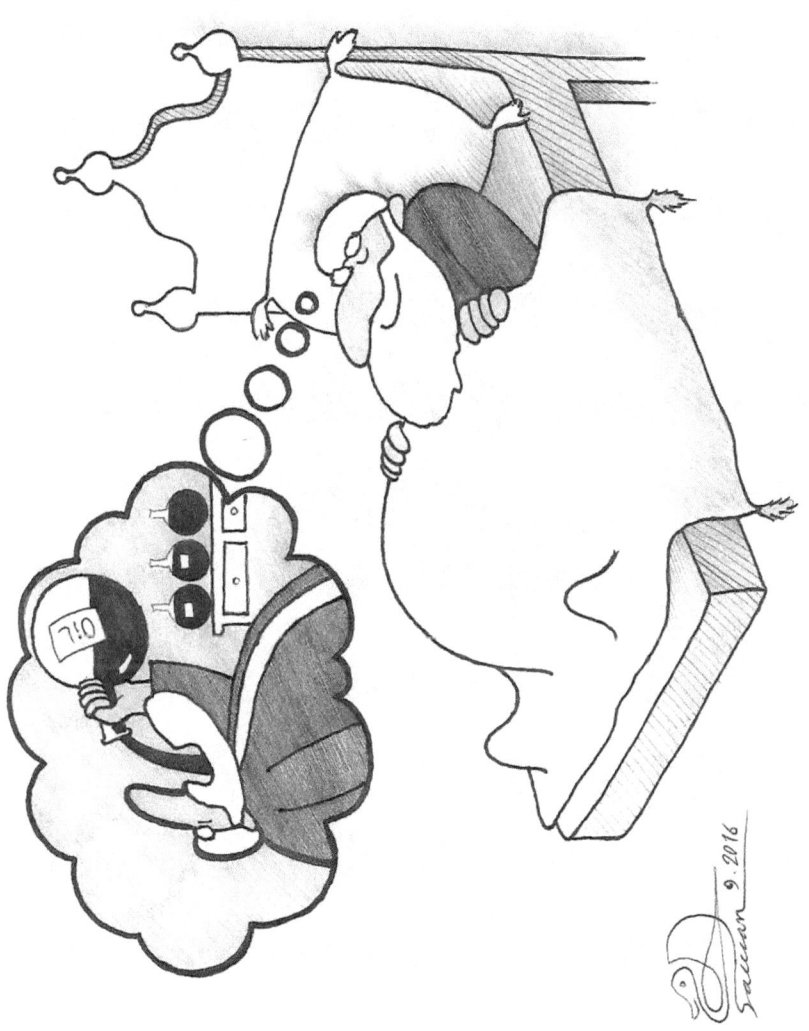

26. WHAT AM I DOING OUT OF IRAN? AM I LOOKING FOR FREEDOME?

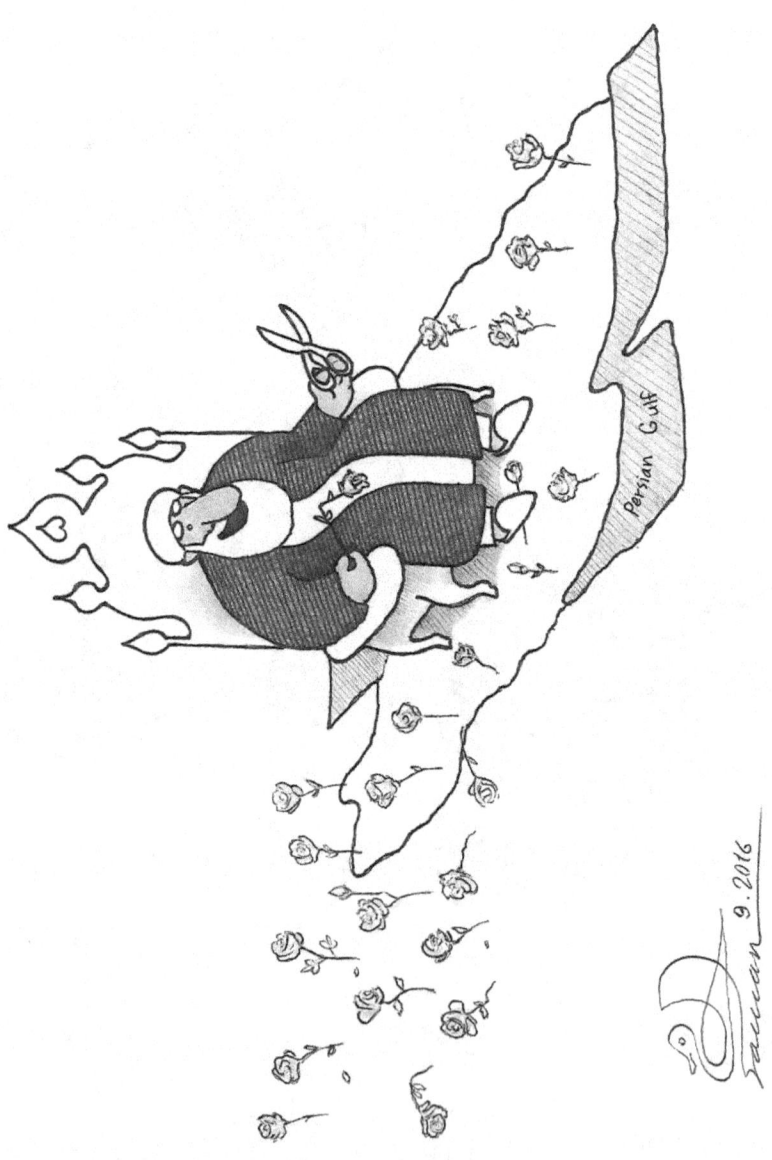

27. GOD KNOWS EVERYTHING. WE NO NEED TO THINK

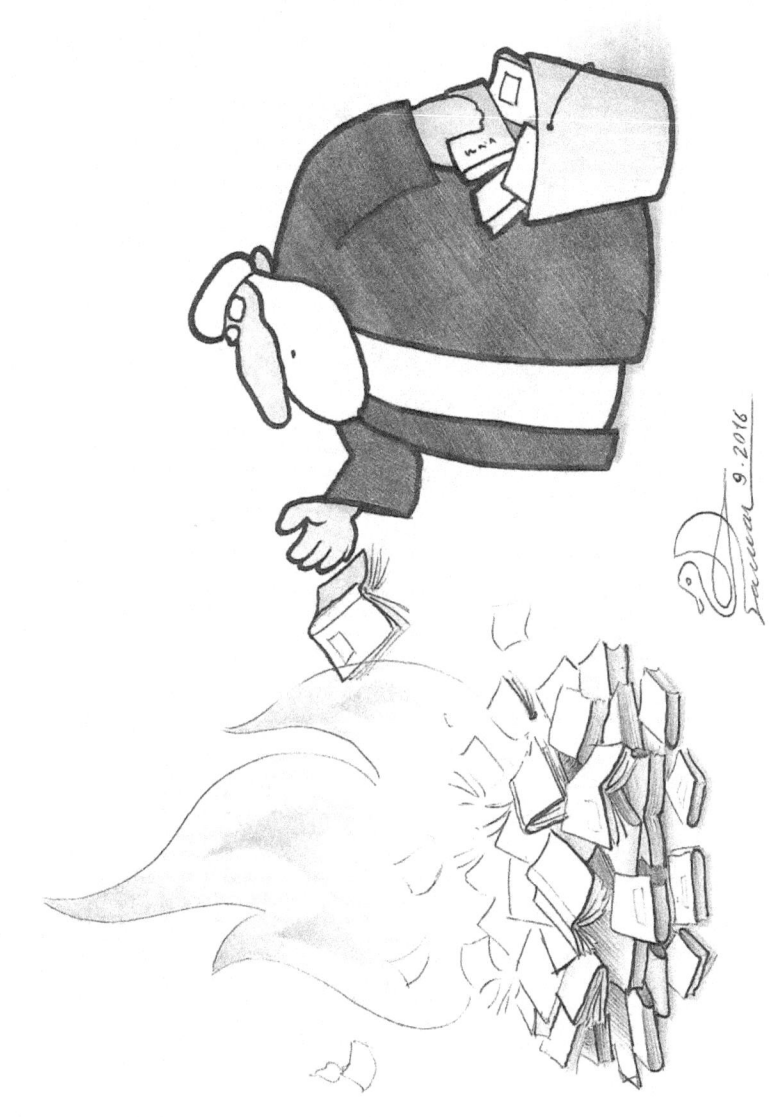

28. HEAVENLY JUSTICE

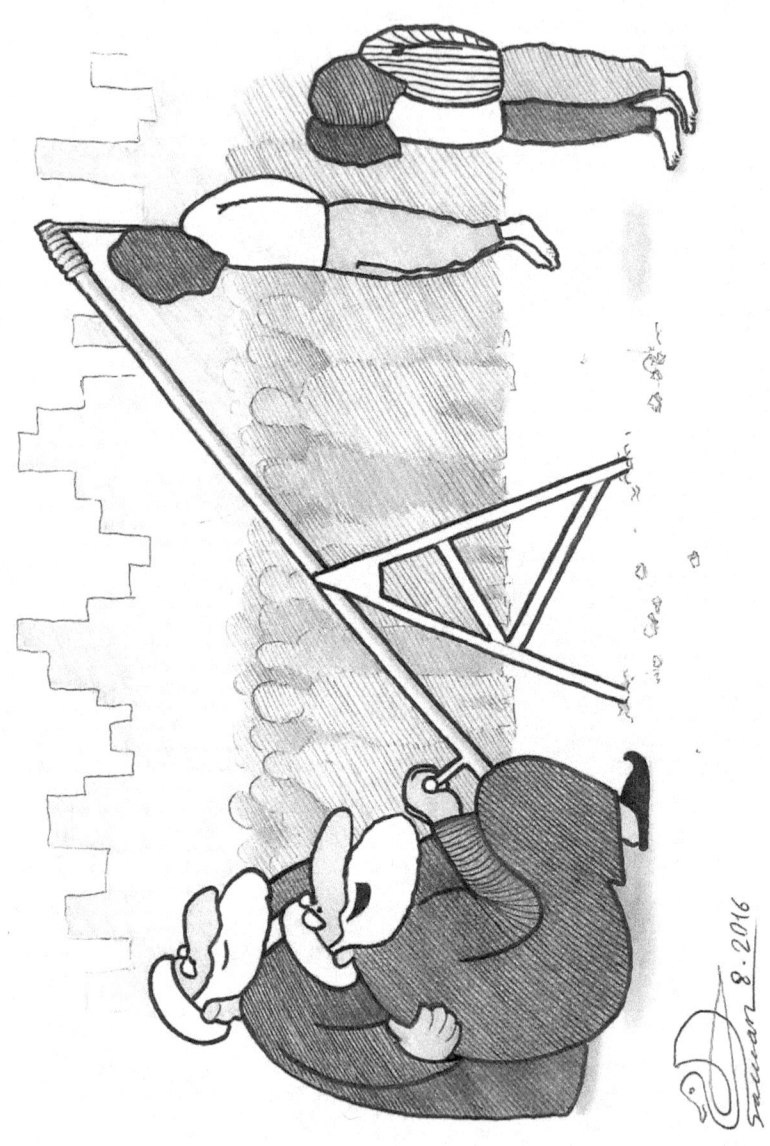

29. THEY NEVER RESPECT THE PEOPLE

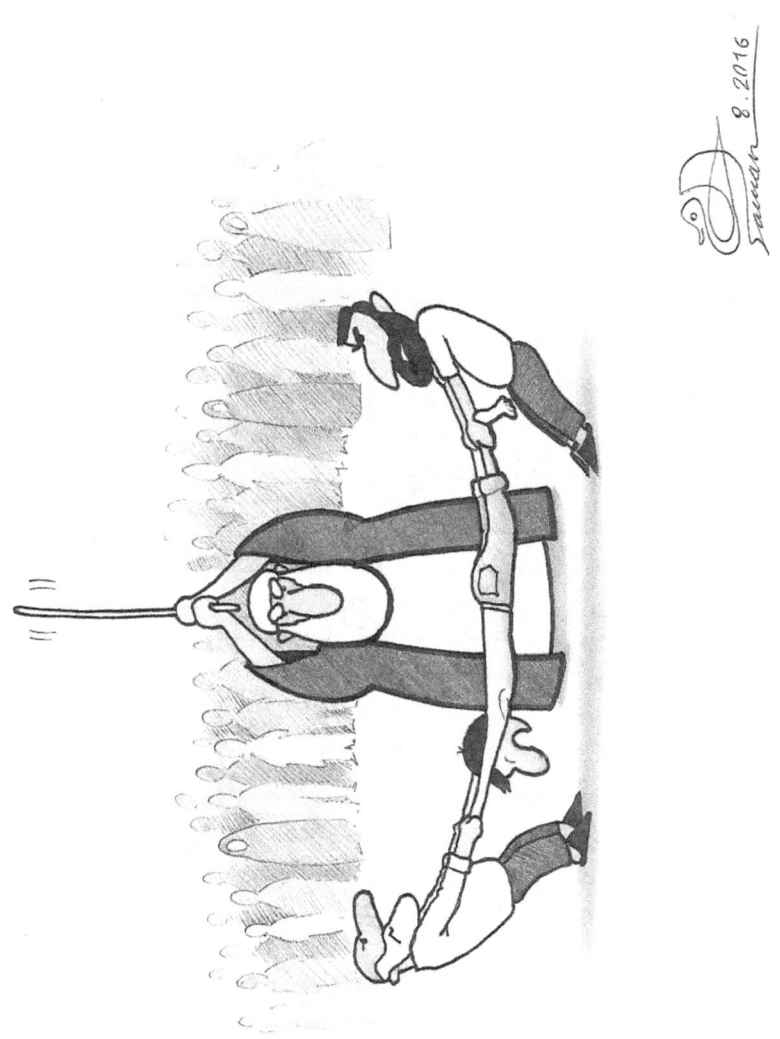

30. PROHIBITED; I FORGOT MY COUNTRY

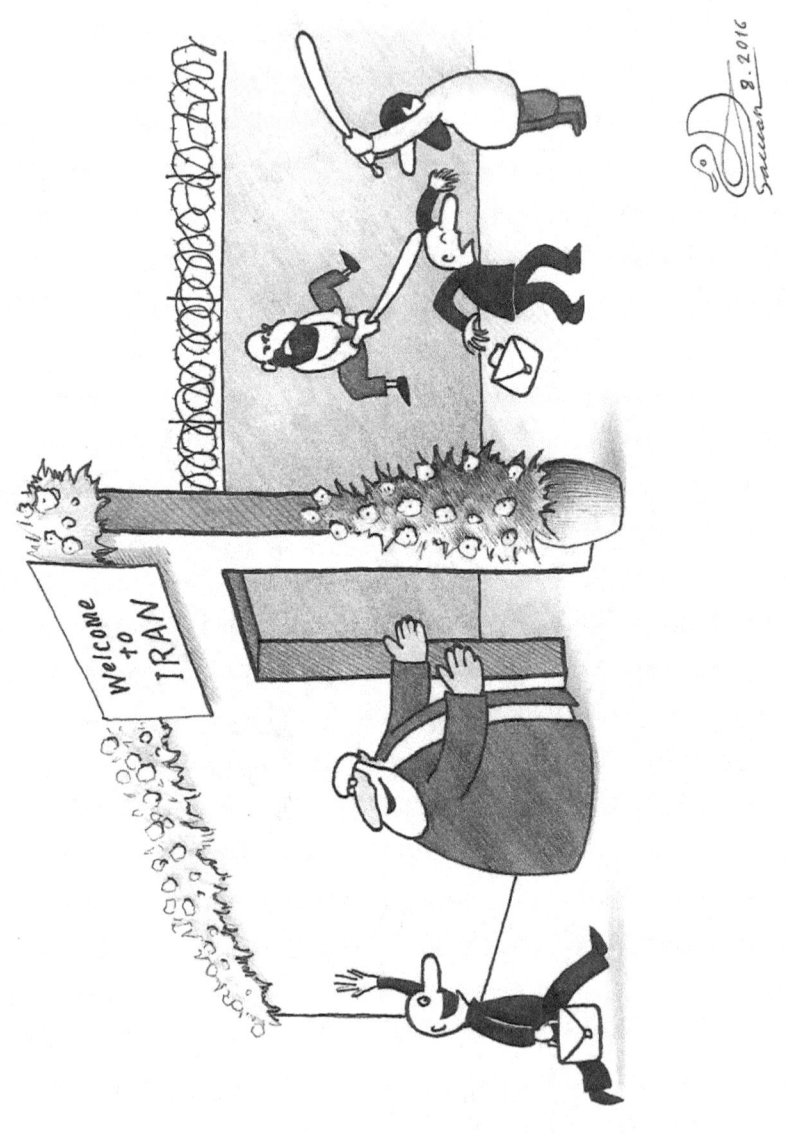

31. DISUNITY

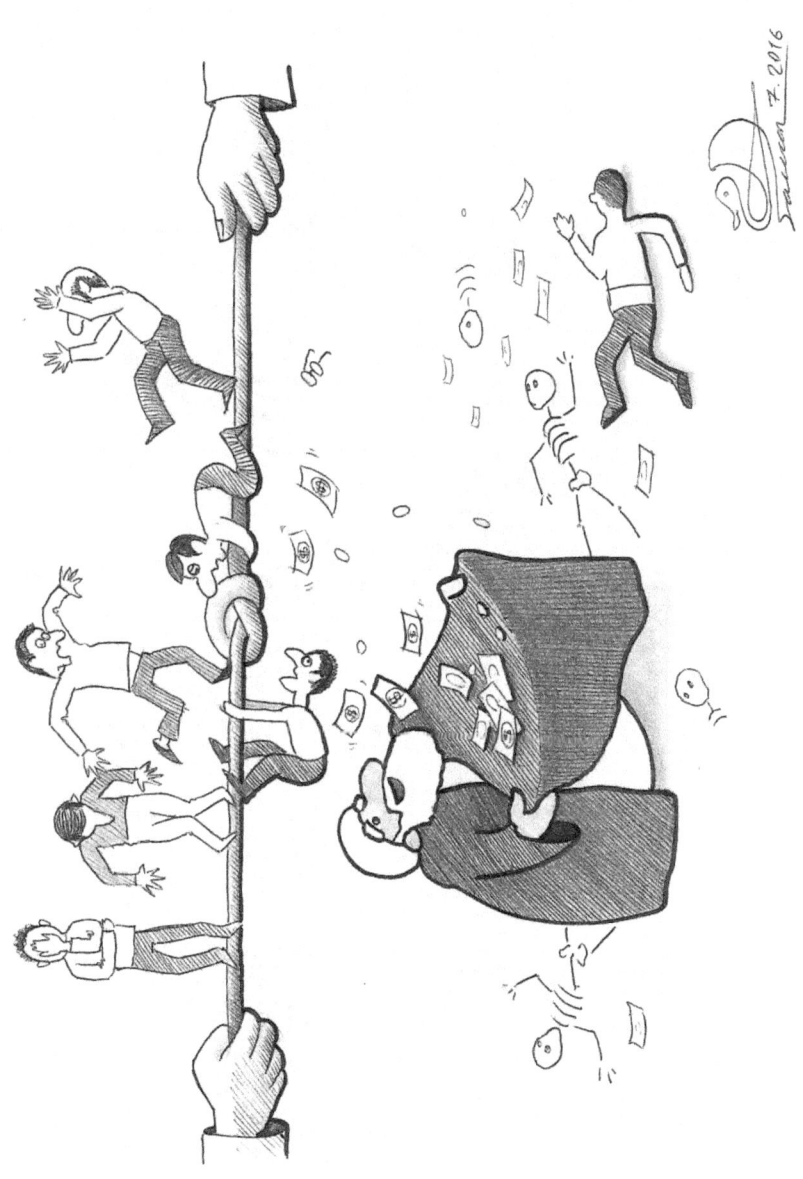

32. A THEATER CALLED: VOTING

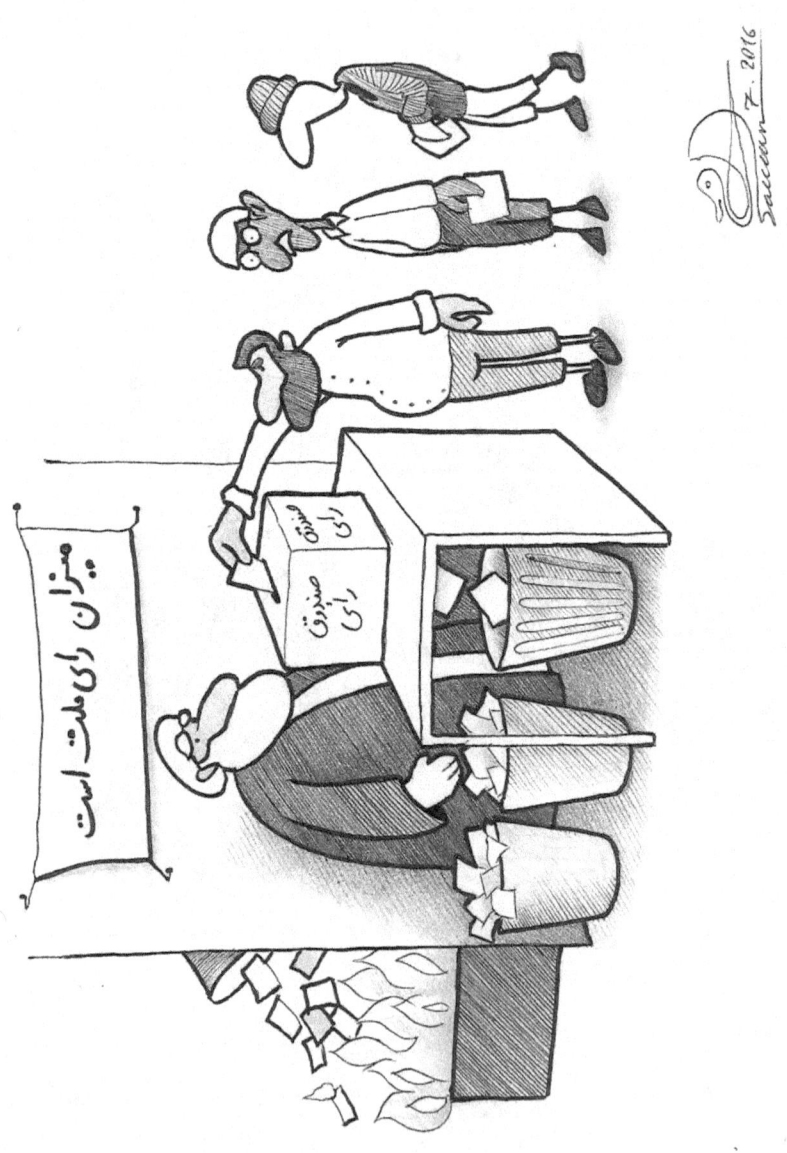

33....!!!

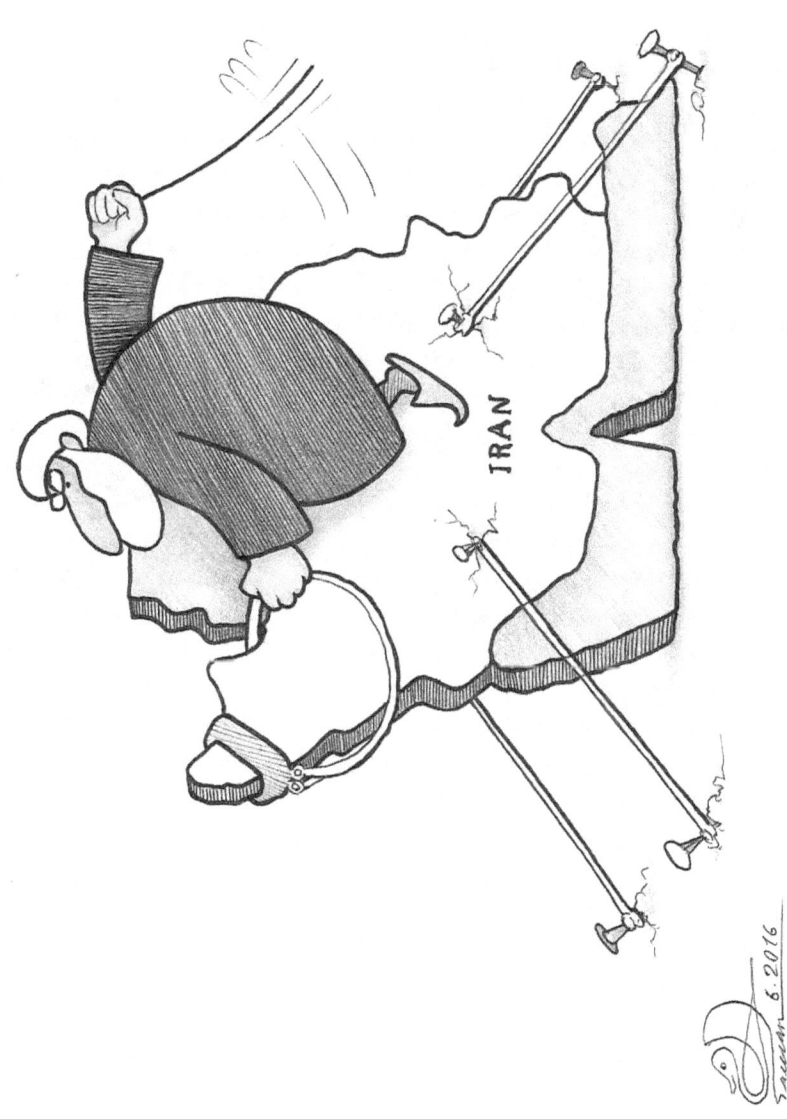

34. THEIR CHILDREN STADY AT WESTERN UNIVERSITIES. BUT THEY CAMPAIGN AGAINST WESTERN POWERS.

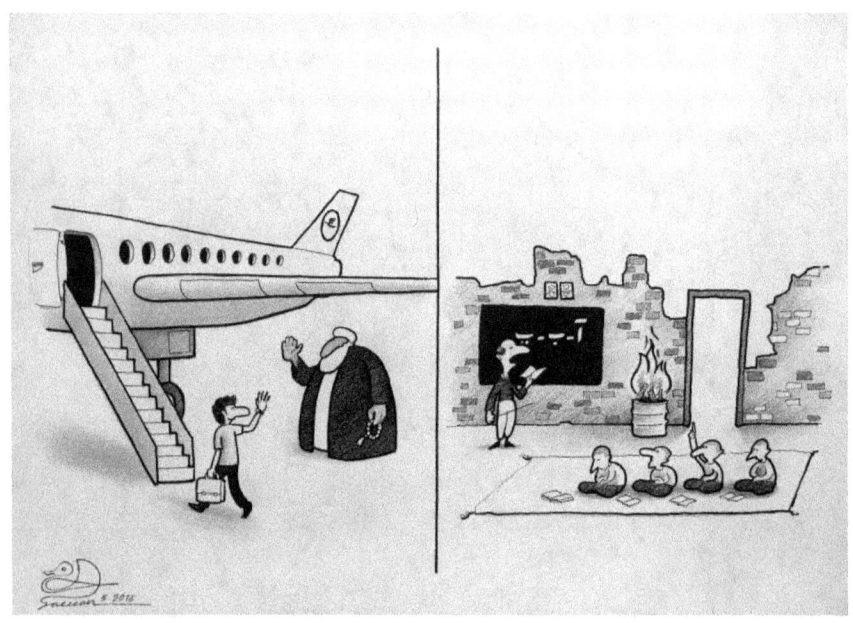

35. ROCKETS AGAINST ISRAEL (SHEHAB 3)

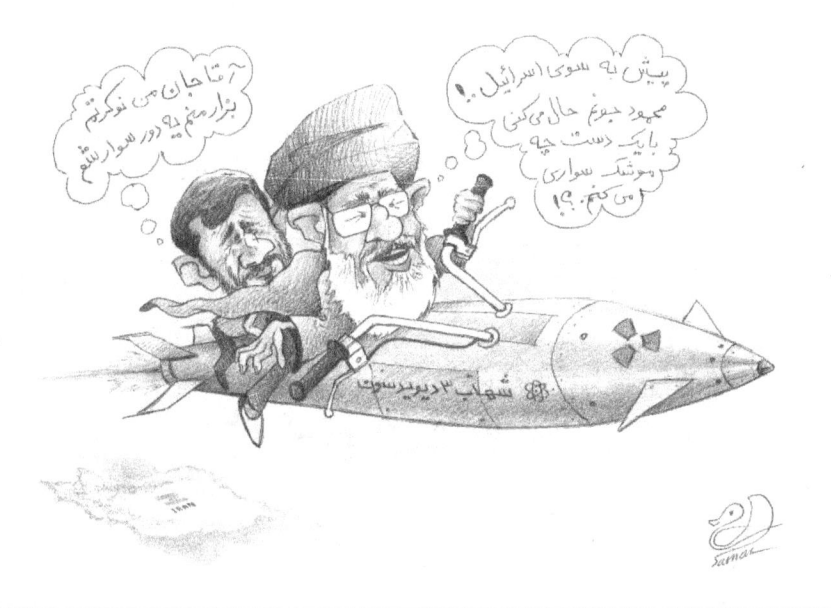

36....!!!??? DEMAGOGUERY

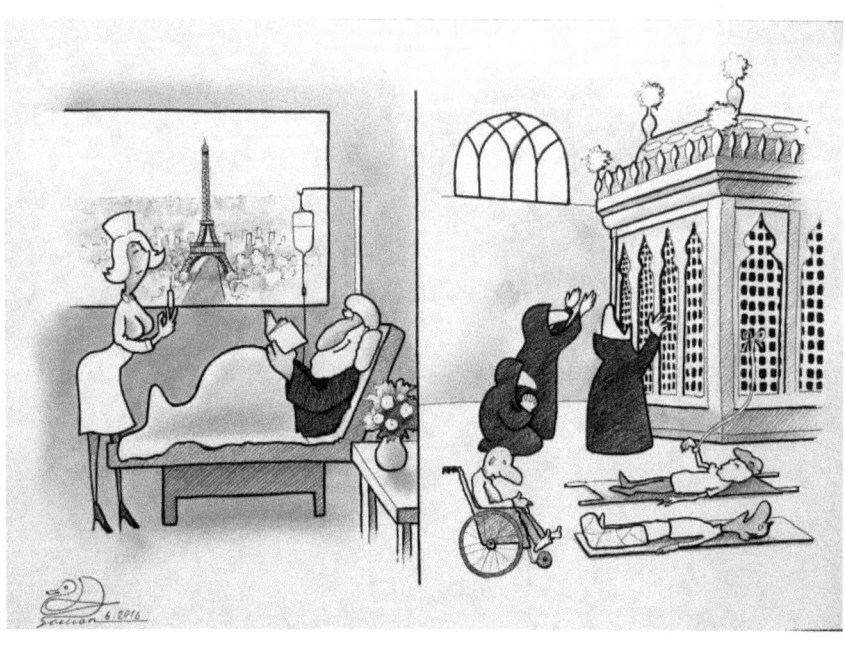

37...!!

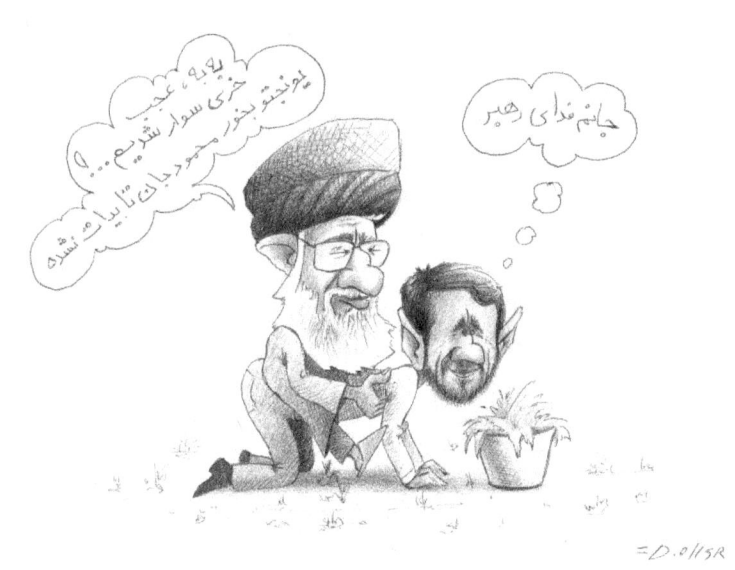

38. HANGING

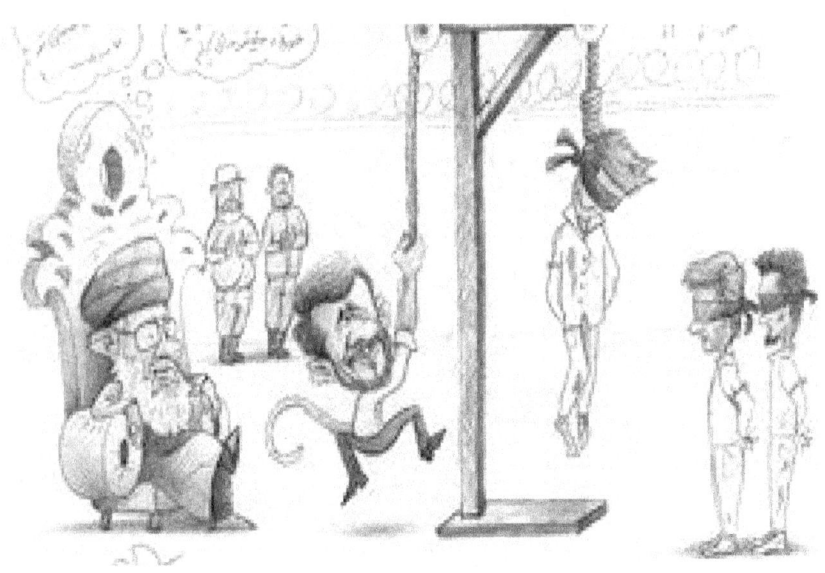

39. AKBAR HASHEMI RAFSANJANI; VICTIM

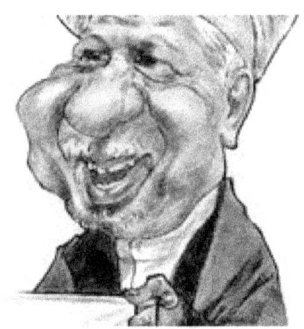

40. THEY FEED THEMSELVES WITH OIL

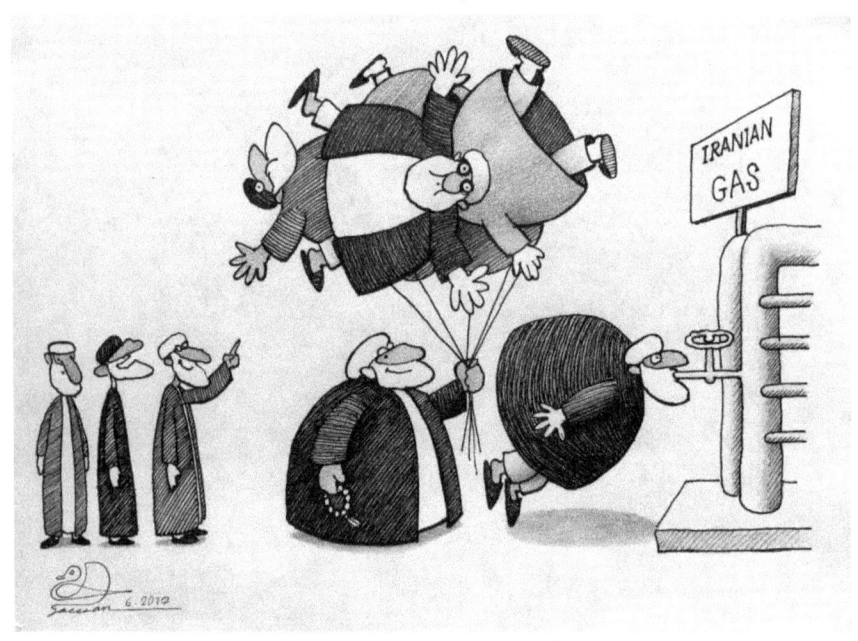

41....!!!

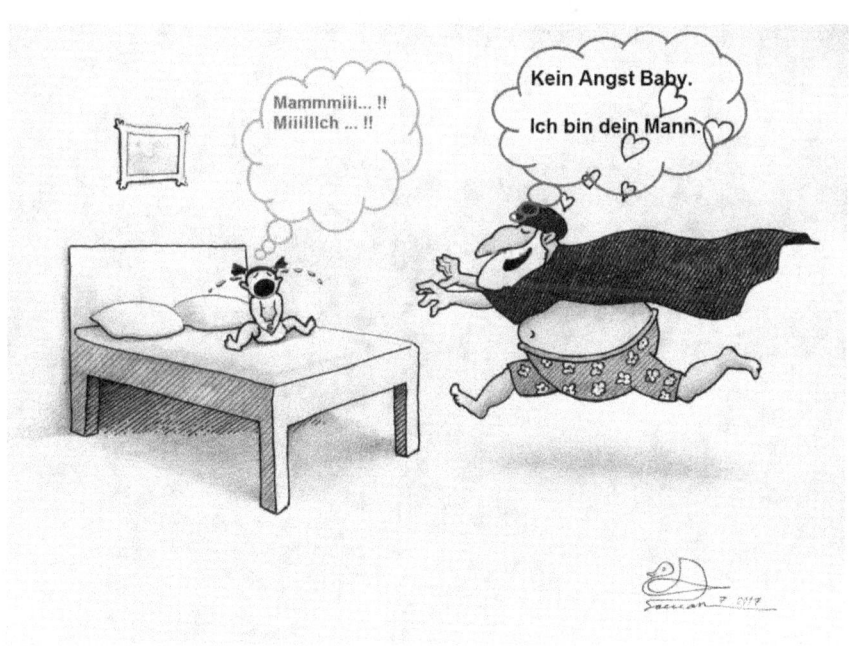

42. IRAN HAS TO BE FREE

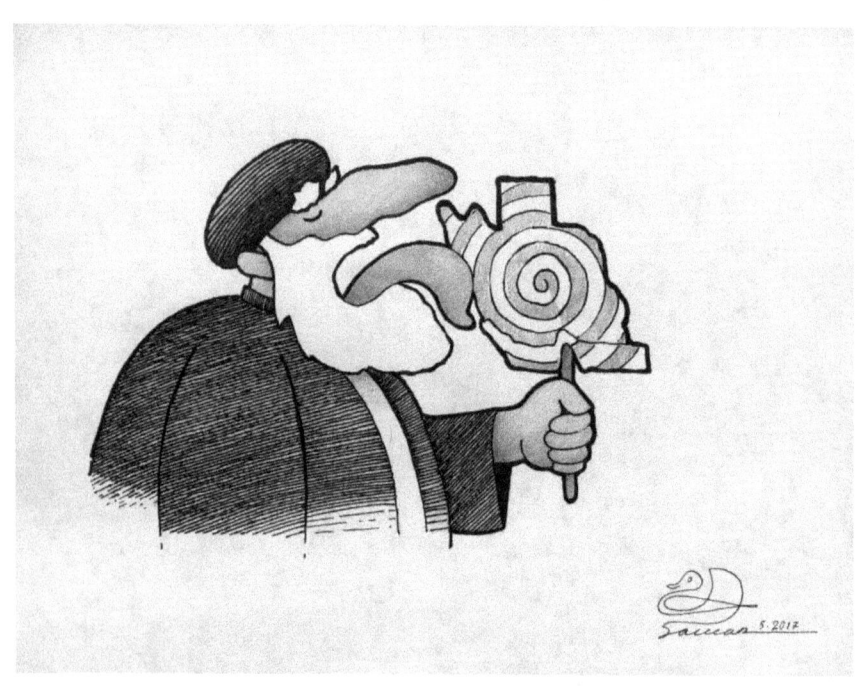

43. HOLIDAY IN IRAN AND CONTROL

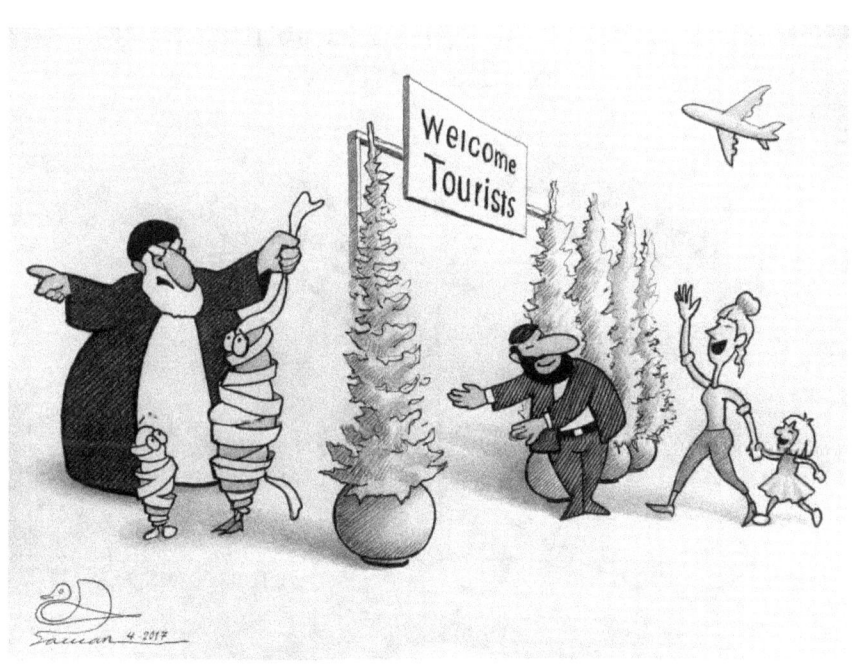

44. GOD SAYS: 'OTHER PEOPLE ARE MORE IMPORTANT'

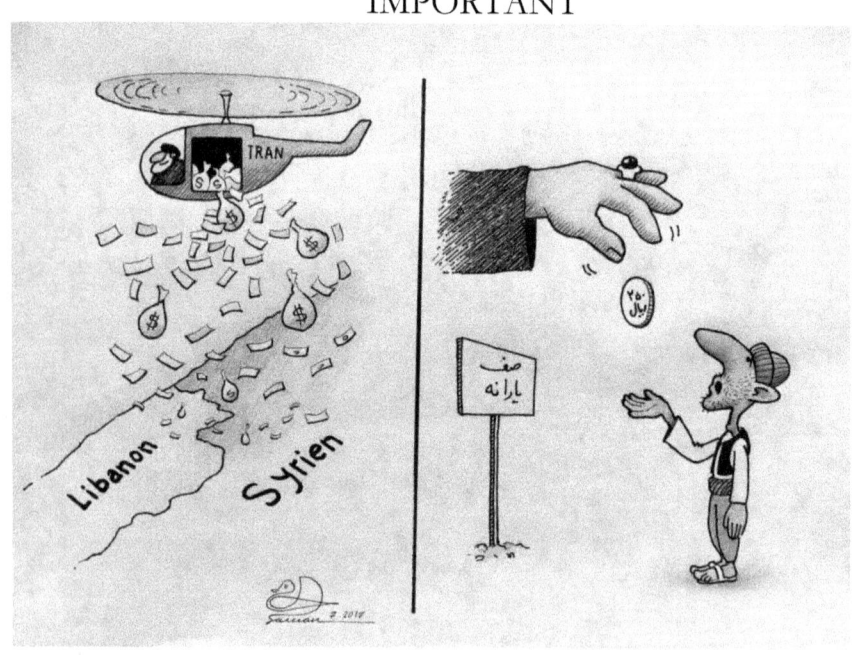

45. OUR IRAN GETS A GRAVE

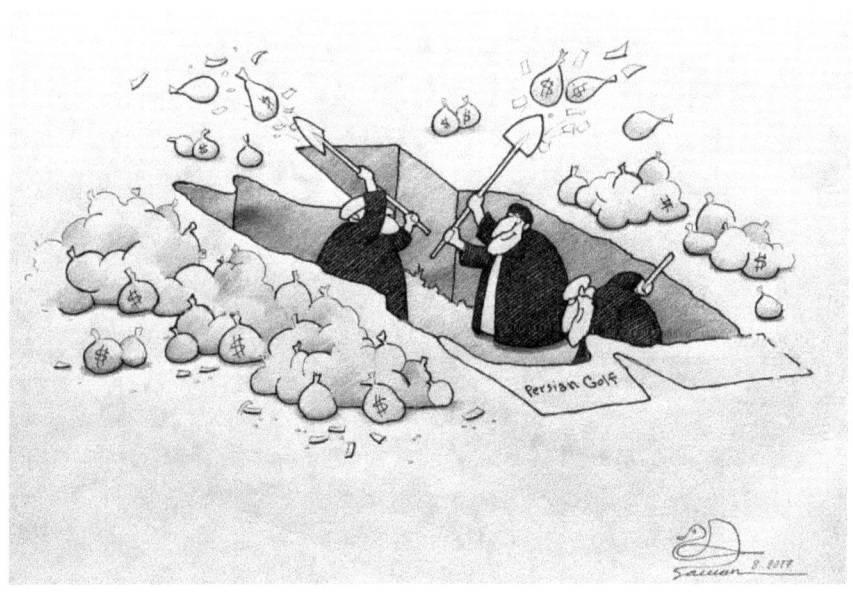

46. THE ISLAMIC POLITICS

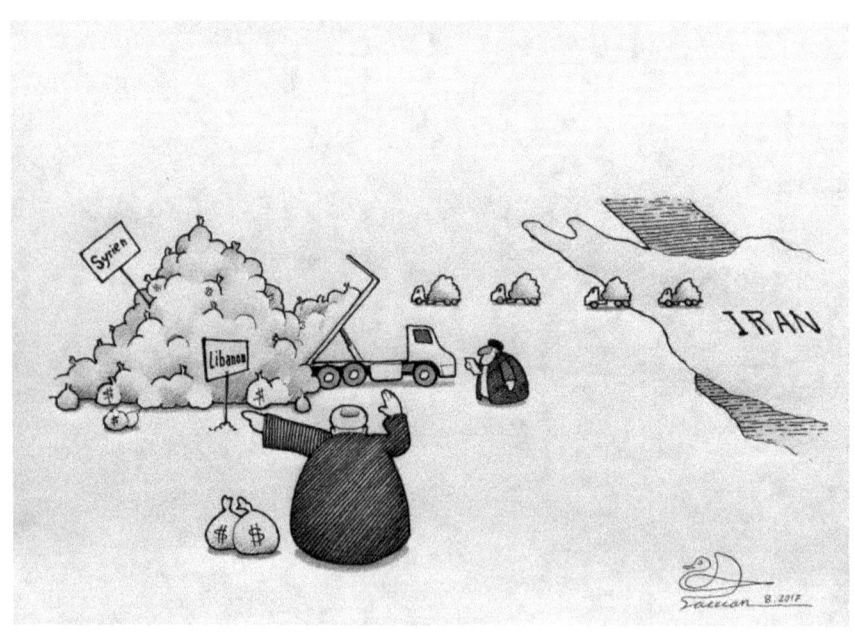

47. LEBANON , SYRIA AND … !

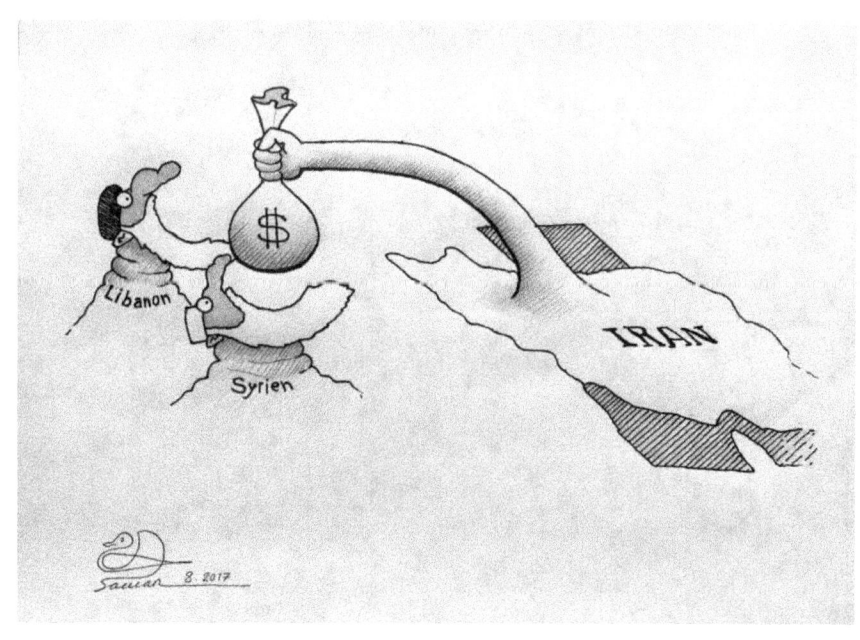

www.ingramcontent.com/pod-product-compliance
Lightning Source LLC
Chambersburg PA
CBHW050025230526
45470CB00003B/1136